Runes
Learn Everything about Runes, Celtic Religions and Celtic History
3rd Edition (2017)

Sarah Thompson

© **Copyright 2017 - All rights reserved.**

In no way is it legal to reproduce, duplicate, or transmit any part of this document in either electronic means or in printed format. Recording of this publication is strictly prohibited and any storage of this document is not allowed unless with written permission from the publisher. All rights reserved. MJG Publishing.

The information provided herein is stated to be truthful and consistent, in that any liability, in terms of inattention or otherwise, by any usage or abuse of any policies, processes, or directions contained within is the solitary and utter responsibility of the recipient reader. Under no circumstances will any legal responsibility or blame be held against the publisher for any reparation, damages, or monetary loss due to the information herein, either directly or indirectly.

Respective authors own all copyrights not held by the publisher.

Legal Notice:

This book is copyright protected. This is only for personal use. You cannot amend, distribute, sell, use, quote or paraphrase any part or the content within this book without the consent of the author or copyright owner. Legal action will be pursued if this is breached.

Disclaimer Notice:

Please note, the information contained within this document is for educational and entertainment purposes only. Every attempt has been made to provide accurate, up to date and reliable complete information. No warranties of any kind are expressed or implied. Readers acknowledge that the author is not engaging in the rendering of legal, financial, medical or professional advice.

By reading this document, the reader agrees that under no circumstances are we responsible for any losses, direct or indirect, which are incurred as a result of the use of information contained within this document, including, but not limited to, — errors, omissions, or inaccuracies.

Disclaimer

All rights reserved. No part of this publication may be reproduced, distributed, or transmitted in any form or by any means, including photocopying, recording, or other electronic or mechanical methods, without the prior written permission of the publisher, except in the case of brief quotations embodied in critical reviews and certain other noncommercial uses permitted by copyright law

Table of Contents

Introduction 7
Chapter 1 What Are Runes? 11
Chapter 2 History Of Runes 21
Chapter 3 Symbols And Meanings 27
Chapter 4 Uses 65
Chapter 5 Runes And Magic 71
Chapter 6 Celtic History 79
Chapter 7 Celtic Religion 113
Conclusion 135
Check Out My Other Books 137
We hope you like it! 139

Introduction

Many people have heard the word runes and yet few actually know what these are or even what their uses are. That is okay as this book will help you to understand the origins, history, and uses of these mysterious items and how in a lot of ways these have come a long way in guiding many people down the road of life and have helped them to understand a lot of the things in their lives that may not have made the most sense to them.

While the exact origins of runes can't be narrowed down, there is a general history of these being used hundreds and thousands of years ago in many regions of the world. These have been thought to be guiding lights in helping people to make sense of their future and guide them in important decision-making attempts. Early runes have also been used in some geographical regions, such as ancient rural Sweden, probably for strictly decorative purposes.

Runes were an integral part of ancient life. They were used to maintain a record of all the knowledge the people of that era were able to accumulate. They are basically the letters in a set of alphabets. These alphabets were known as runic alphabets. They were the foundation of many Germanic languages. Then along came the Latin alphabet that took on a more specialized approach and gradually phased out the runes.

The study of runic inscriptions, runic alphabets, runestones, and their history, is collectively known as runology. Today, runology forms a specialized branch of Germanic linguistics. The earliest records of runes date back to 150AD. Following Christianization, the runes were phased out as the Romans favored using Latin alphabets more than runes. Even after this attempt at phasing runes out, they continued to exist in northern and central Europe. They were in circulation until about the end of the twentieth century as they were used to decorate stuff and to make runic calendars. Among the runic alphabets, three are very well known. They are Elder Futhark, Anglo-Saxon Futhorc, and

Younger Futhark. Historically speaking, the runic alphabet is derived from the Old Italian alphabets. The oldest inscriptions having runes were found in north Germany and Denmark.

With the study of runes and all things associated with the topic, there has been, and still is, a large amount of interest in the topic that gives a lot of people the guidance that they have been seeking out. While the subject of runes is a large and expansive one, this book will hopefully be a good place for you to jumpstart your study into this topic and help you to get a better understanding of something that has baffled a large part of the world's population. With all of this being said, let's begin our journey into the history of runes, what they are exactly, and where they came from.

Chapter 1
What Are Runes?

There is a short and a long answer to that question. In short, runes are the letters that are contained in a series of related alphabets that all form what is known as a runic language. There are those that suggest that, as well as being used as a source of communication, there is another use for runes in the form of magic.

Runes, as you will discover in this book, have a lot of other uses. They're used for writing, as well as to take on many different purposes in the magical world. It's imperative to note that the fortune of a person cannot be told by runes, but they are a good way to help a person see the path they are currently traveling. Knowing this, you will be able to travel the path and proceed in the direction that you want to take. You'll be able to make massive adjustments or stay the course.

In a later chapter, I will introduce you to a use that has been explored but is not a popular utilization of this tool.

But really, what are runes other than a language and a tool to be used for magic? Where did they come from?

Runes date back to around 150 A.D. The Germanic peoples who lived from the 1st and 2nd centuries A.D. used runes for a variety of purposes, including linguistic.

Who were the Germanic peoples? 'Germanic' is a general term that has seen frequent use by scholars and scribes since times of antiquity to describe a multitude of tribal cultures. Specifically, Roman scribes used the term 'Germanic' to refer to the tribes that inhabited the regions of Lower, Upper and Greater Germania—these regions correspond roughly to modern-day Luxembourg, Alsace, the Netherlands, Belgium, the North of France, and, as its name suggests, Germany.

These tribes were viewed by these same Roman historians as

being physically hardier, but far less civilized and couth than themselves. Also importantly, Germanic groups were considered distinct from the Celtic Gauls, who were considered to be less advanced than the Romans, but still a step above the Germanic peoples.

The use of runes is believed to have been spread by cultural contact between Germanic people, who often traveled widely abroad as mercenaries in the Roman army and throughout the Italian peninsula during the 1st century BC to the 5th century AD.

Historians speculate that the popular use of runes may have spread during the late Common Germanic stage. While it might be tempting to regard the runes carved by early peoples to be simple creations depicting a crude language, we now know that even the earliest runes, while lacking clear phonetic and linguistic complexity, reveal a rich diaspora of dialects. Indeed, the earliest runes made by the Germanic people incorporate a dazzling tapestry of dialects that would continue to diversify in later centuries, such as North Germanic, West Germanic, and Eastern Germanic.
There were a number of different systems developed, but they were replaced around 700 A.D. with the Latin alphabet we're currently using today

The term *'runes'* is used to distinguish these early symbols from the Latin and Greek letters we commonly use today. 'Rune' has its origins in the Germanic root *run*, or the Gothic *runa*. To scholars, the meaning of runa is at once symbolic and tantalizing, translating roughly to "secret," or "whisper" in many early Germanic dialects. For instance, in Welsh and Old English, the word *rhin* or *rūn* has connotations of "mystery" and "secret" and, in some cases, "secret writing".

In Old Irish Gaelic, the word *rún* means "secret" or "secret intention," and if one were to go even further back in time, the modern English word "rune" can be seen to have been loaned from the Proto-Germanic word *rūnō, meaning "secret letter" or "secret literature." From its earliest inception, the very idea of runes was deeply steeped in a sense of mystery and wonder. So it should come as no surprise that the early peoples would associate runes with intrigue, mysticism, and a kind of secret wisdom available only to those who could decipher them.

The legend that surrounds these runes begins with the Norse God Odin. It is said that the runes were a gift from the Gods to Odin after a wound inflicted upon him by his own hand by a spear. He hung himself from the World Tree, Yggdrasil, for nine days in order to learn the secret language of the runes. This experience came to be popularly known as Odin's ordeal to learn the secrets of the runes. It is said Odin himself described his experience in great detail in his poem. He penned the epic poem, *Havamal,* which describes in great detail Odin's personal perspective of that horrible experience.

While the legend of Odin's suffering and ordeal does a great deal to elaborate on the mystical significance and power that the ancient Scandinavians attributed to runes, it does not really explain the real world origins of runes. This fact still eludes modern scholars, although several prominent theories have been formulated; we will examine these theories in greater depth in later chapters. Historians do seem to have formed a relative consensus that runes probably had some historical basis on the Old Italic alphabets.

The term 'Old Italic' refers to one of several alphabet systems that saw widespread use in the Italian Peninsula during ancient times, several hundred years before the rise of the Germanic runic alphabet. Numerous Old Italic alphabet systems existed, each used by a different indigenous group, and each representing their specific Indo-European language. For instance, the Sabellians, Oscan, Umbrian, Celtic, Venetic, and Messapic peoples used a form of Old Italic, whereas the Faliscan, North Picene, and other peoples inhabiting the Oscan and Umbrian regions used an alphabet form more closely derived from the Etruscan variant of Old Italic. However, just which of the Old Italic alphabets gave birth to Germanic runes is a question that is still hotly debated by linguistic scholars.

An interesting characteristic of Germanic runes is that its

characters contain absolutely no horizontal strokes: only vertical and diagonal strokes are used in rendering each symbol of this alphabet. There is a practical historical basis for this. Since wood or stone were the favored materials upon which to carve runes, vertical and diagonal strokes produced more legible and aesthetically pleasing symbols. Horizontal strokes would go along the grain, and would thus produce runes that were less readable, and threatened to weaken or even split the wood.

Possibly the most interesting realization that historians have made about runes is that, in its earliest forms, they were not, in fact, used as a writing system at all. To date, the earliest examples of runic inscriptions found on artifacts sometimes bore simple messages, such as the name of the craftsman who made the artifact, or who it belonged to.

However, there are other longer sequences of runes that continue to baffle linguistic theorists and confound attempts to decipher their meaning. It has been theorized that these sequences hint that runes, in its earliest form, were not widely used, or perhaps even used at all, for recording messages, but instead, as magical signs. Historians have reasoned that the earliest runes were tools that were used with one purpose in mind. They were solely used for divination and for opening up psychic awareness. It stands to reason that, with the fact that the various meanings of the word rune all translate to meanings associated with "secret," "mystery," and "hidden things", runes were originally imbued with a distinctly esoteric value. Their appearance was rare, and possibly highly valued, because they were restricted to a particular elite, perhaps shaman, wise men, or other mystics who learned or were taught how to carve and read them.

Runes are a set of twenty-four stones or tiles containing primitive carvings of letters or characters. These runes can be implemented to gain spiritual insight and messages. They provide another alternative for conversing with the universe and your higher self.

As we mentioned earlier, the word itself, rune, translates to something hidden or secret, and there is plenty of evidence that dates from the Germanic Iron Age and Roman period to show that they were originally used for magical purposes. They appear on amulets in order to act as charms from these time periods. There is a sixth-century warning on a monument from the Master of the Runes that he hid powerful runes inside the monument, and anyone who dared to damage the monument would die. This monument is the Stentoften Runestone, found in the province of Blekinge, Sweden, and the curse it bears has been an important key for modern historians in their attempts to understand the significance of runes to the early Germanic people. Perhaps the fact that the Stentoften Runestone is still standing—no less in the same spot where it was first erected hundreds upon hundreds of years ago—is a testament to the ominous power and magic behind the runes that bear the curse of the Master of Runes!

Even as late as the medieval period, runes were associated with mystic potency and magical significance. A prime example of this is the Franks Casket, also known as the Auzon Casket, an artifact which has generated considerable interest in the scholarly world. Made from whale's bone, the casket is decorated with impeccably intricate illustrations and runes. What makes the Franks Casket particularly striking to the academic community is that it is decorated with imagery, symbolism, and runic alphabets from a variety of contrasting cultures: Germanic, Roman, and even Christian? The complexity of the rune languages and illustrations imply that the casket was a prized creation indeed, possibly meant as a tribute gifted to a king or other great leader.

For centuries, runes were only used and known by an elite few and only began to become popular around the 1980s. During that time, an entire series of books, sets, and cards were created in order to reveal how they could be utilized for magical and divinatory purposes. Many people began their psychic path using runes as their inspiration.

For divinatory exploits, they hold a lot in similarity to the I-Ching. They are usually stored in a bag just like the I-Ching. When required, they are drawn out one after the other and cast on a flat surface, where they can be interpreted by an expert or a rune reader.

Chapter 2
History Of Runes

There are four different theories as to the creation of the runes. There's the Roman Theory, Indigenous Theory, Greek Theory, and North-Italic Theory. Unfortunately, how they were created and how they traversed from one place to the next is not clear to historians today. They could be an adaptation of a previous alphabet, or the result of original work. However, in order to understand these symbols better, you should know the four different theories to the rune creations.

Roman Theory

Presented in 1874 by L.F.A. Wimmer, this theory states that the runes were an adaptation of the Latin alphabet. It's assumed in this theory that the Germanic people came into contact with the Roman culture through the invasion of the Cimbri and Teutones. The Germanic people then became familiar with the Latin alphabet as early as the second century B.C.E. They adapted this alphabet into the runes that we know today and put them to use, spreading them via trade routes into Scandinavian countries and eastward from that point.

However, there is not much evidence that the runes were near the Roman lands at this time. The spread of the runes into the Scandinavian countries and eastward could mean that the adaptation of the Roman alphabet wasn't finished until the runes began to spread north.

Indigenous Theory

First put out there in 1896 by R.M. Meyer and made popular by the National Socialist Germany, this theory says that the runes were the original alphabet. Not only were they the original one, but they also were the groundwork on which the Greeks and Phoenician alphabets were made.

This theory does not hold much ground because the earliest Phoenician works date back to around the thirteenth or twelfth century B.C.E., but the earliest runic inscription only goes back to the first century C.E.

Greek Theory

Shortly after the Indigenous Theory was made known, the Greek Theory came about in 1899 and was introduced by Sophus Bugge. This theory states the ancient Germanic people adopted the Greek alphabet and changed it in order to create the runes. The theory begins with the Goths coming in contact with the cursive form of the Greek alphabet. The Goths adapted this form of the alphabet for their use and it was spread during their travels.

There are some problems with this theory, though, and it has led to the abandonment of the theory by many. The earliest the Goths could have adapted this alphabet was around 200 C.E., and the initial runic inscription would have been earlier than that.

North-Italic Theory

Brought about by C.J.S. Marstrander in 1928, this theory was strengthened by Wolfgang Krause in 1937. The theory begins with the Germanic people living in the Alps and coming in contact with the Etruscan or North-Italic alphabet and adapting it. The Cimbri came in contact with the new alphabet and began to pass it on to the Suevi, who carried the runes up the Rhine River to the North Sea and beyond.

There is one problem with this theory, though. The encounter would have had to take place two or three hundred years before any runic inscriptions were actually dated. This doesn't mean that didn't happen. Items made with wood could have been carved with the runes and decayed.

It is known that runes were used by the Germans for many centuries, and this goes back to 100 B.C. until around 1600 A.D. This was, for a large part, used throughout the majority of Europe, the British Isles, and North America. The use of runes in the North Americas could be evidence that the Vikings discovered the North Americas long before Columbus.

While many say that runes got their start via the Norse lineage of heritage, you don't have to be of Norse heritage to use runes in your everyday life. One person has summed the whole topic of runes up simply by saying that you often will use runes to seek advice on a number of subjects that will come along in the course of your life. There is a bit of advice that can come from these when using them. Detail your particular circumstances and then simply ask your question. If you do this and are specific about the question, this will help to decrease the amount of confusion that will result from asking this question. While it is not a sure thing that you will get the answers that you seek, it is a good place to start in getting the questions you have narrowed down in a lot of ways.

Another thing that you need to understand is that, while

answers may be presented, you still have to sort out the meaning. This is where a rune caster will be handy, as they will be able to read the answers in a way that you may not otherwise have got. Their insight will be key to making sure that you are getting the actual answer that you are seeking and not just seeing the answer that you are wanting in hopes of having the right answer. We will discuss this in a little more detail in later chapters of the book.

As will be touched on in this book later, one interesting aspect that came from the discovery of runes, and which has evolved ever since, was a researcher who one day claimed that he was able to use runes to communicate with the dead. This person swore on all that he believed in that he had successfully communicated with the spirits of a deceased family member and had received closure from this interaction. When he was pushed to provide details and proof of this interaction, he was unable to do so and as a result was dismissed as not being very reliable. There have since been a number of these people who have claimed to be able to do this as well, and yet there has not been any real proof of this ability.

Chapter 3
Symbols And Meanings

When talking about runes and their meanings, there is a large amount of information that is out there to pull from. In the interest of keeping this book from being long and hard to read, we will take all of this information and break it all down into one chapter that will be easy to digest and will also be very informative as well as entertaining. We will look at many runes and explain their meanings to help you get a better understanding and clear up a lot of the confusion that comes from time to time.

One thing that needs to be remembered is that there are many variations of the alphabet and that these forms have their own variations of the alphabet. It is very important that you make sure that you do not mix these up, as their meanings will become confused and clouded. For this article we will talk about the more popular of these, the Elder Futharks. The Elder is the only part of the name that will vary from type to type, as the collection of the runes is known as a Futhark.

Among the Germanic tribes, the Elder Futhark is the oldest form of runic alphabets, surviving in the form of the great standing runestones in Scandinavia, as well as a variety of jewelry, amulets, tools and weapons dating back to the 2nd to 8th centuries. The term 'Futhark' is named after the initial sounds of the first six rune names: F, U, Th, A, R, and K.

When dealing with Futharks, it is vital that you know that these are broken down into groups of eight. This is done for a couple of reasons. The first is that the person in question will be able to remember their order, and the next reason for that is due to the fact that the order does in a lot of ways have an impact on the significance that it has in the terms of magic use.

Fehu

Fehu has the 'f' sound and stands for cattle. Its colors are green and brown. Fehu represents power and control. It signifies a new beginning and a movable wealth like credit or money. It's a rune that gives the bearer power they need in order to get wealthy, as well as the power they need in order to hold onto it. Its divinatory meanings include money, wealth, prosperity goals, self-esteem, centeredness, karma, promotions, and concerns with physical and financial needs. The magical uses are limited to money, promotion, and business, finding a job, achieving a goal and starting new enterprises.

A quick analysis will show us that Fehu has an important role in the day-to-day realities of our lives. It also enlightens us to whatever lies beyond, by acting as a catalyst. It is usually whatever we think we are. However, it frequently bears no resemblance to what we eventually stand to find. It also has a purpose, as it is our home. After all our wanderings and experiences, we do need a way to ground ourselves both physically and emotionally. This is usually done by allowing oneself to enjoy the simple pleasures of home, good work, and family.

Fehu is very vital in reminding us that we should be well

anchored in our physical condition before we attempt embarking upon any spiritual endeavor. All of us have accepted at some point the mundane reality of our lives. Sadly, not many people ever see the world beyond this stage. So it would not be farfetched to say that they have become as docile and domesticated as regular cattle. They live their everyday lives as usual, without having any ambitions for anything more than normal. Sometimes, they are not even aware of what other possibilities lay in store for them. The first step that each person should take to actually overcome this is to be brave enough to take a peek at what lies in store, without worrying about what they stand to lose if they choose that option.

Uruz

ᚢ

Uruz has the sound 'oo' and represents the auroch or wild ox. Its colors are dark green and orange. It is also the rune of power, but it's a power that we are unable to control or own. In a casting, this rune can mean that personal success is close. For charms and talismans, it's used for healing. Its divinatory meanings are passion, instinct, vitality, fertility, sexuality, wildness, irrationality, Rite of Passage, Shamanic Experience. And the unconscious primitive mind. The magical uses are spread over things like strengthening the will and increasing sexual energy and potency.

As mentioned earlier, Uruz represents an animal called auroch. These creatures were very similar to bison and used to be a common sight all around Europe. They were believed to be just shy of elephants in size and they had tusks as long as six feet. These tusks were in high demand by the Germanii as drinking horns. An auroch hunt was also considered to be a rite of passage for a boy entering manhood. Aurochs were the height of wild animals. This is a stark contrast when compared to the domesticated cattle depicted by Fehu.

Uruz also has the honor of being the rune representing the God of the sacred hunt and his shaman/priest. Reflecting on the usual mundane and routine life, Uruz would be the first attempt that man made to control the divine in nature by the use of sympathetic magic. It also reminds us of impending death and our mortality. It is one of the traits that distinguishes us from other animals. The energy of this rune is unadulterated and powerful in the sense that it is distinctly masculine. It symbolizes the journey of the boy who took the rite of passage to enter into manhood. The boy who felled the aurochs was considered to have pitched himself into the first level of mysteries. He had learnt that the source of life is death.

Thurisaz

Thruisaz has the sound 'th' and stands for giant or thorn. Its color is white. This rune signifies the ability to resist an unwanted conflict with being passive. It's a rune of protection and can tell the drawer of a possible change that could come without warning. For charms and talismans, it's used as a defense against adversaries. Its divinatory meanings are painful events, discipline, hardship, knowledge, introspection, and focus. The magical uses of Thruisaz are aiding in study and meditation, clearing out a bad situation, and self-discipline.

This rune is very special, as it is the first of the "obstacle" runes. Contrary to what the name might suggest, these runes are not destructive in nature. They are placed in our path so that we learn from them. They strengthen us and teach us to overcome hardships. The main idea that the rune seeks to impart is that you must suffer so that you can learn. Apart from the literal meaning of the phrase, we also have to allow our destiny to unravel and experience everything that life has to offer us. Appearances can be extremely deceptive. What may appear to be a negative and harrowing experience could actually be a life lesson in disguise. This analogy can be extended to the giants. They may bring about destruction and may seem very evil at first glance, but they bring about change and eventually clear a route for the new age.

Ansuz

ᚨ

The sound of ansuz is 'aa' or 'aah' and it stands for divine breath or mouth. The color is purple. This rune signifies stability and order. It's a rune that indicates an intellectual activity and represents the divine breath of life and creation. Ansuz stands for Odin. It portrays a leader, authority figure, justice, clairvoyant, shaman, and mind and body balance. It is also used for some magical purposes, mainly for success, leadership, for wise decisions, and to help in divination and magic. This rune describes the primal and instinctive energy of the uruz, tempered with the experience and discipline of purisaz. Odin's personage shows a combination of these elements, exhibiting the characteristics of both chieftain and shaman and being a god of wisdom as well as war. Unknown to most people, Odin is also a shaman. He travels between the worlds on his eight-legged horse, Sleipnir.

This rune also has the specialty of being a balanced rune. Similar to Fehu, most people make the choice to remain stagnant at this point of their lives. It stands for power; power that is both secular and magical. This power can be extremely seductive. Odin had learned the wisdom the first three runes had to offer. This made him a very wise ruler, capable of ruling extremely well, but that was only another beginning. In retrospection, he has gained only temporal power and he has only a few of the tools required to perfect himself spiritually. In spite of everything, this rune lacks perspective and compassion. Although Odin sits high above the world, looking down upon the world and making big decisions, he lacks the capacity to understand the world or himself for that matter. The only thing that is keeping him from becoming a truly great leader is an emotional connection.

Raidho

Raidho is represented by the sound 'r' and represents the cartwheel or wheel. Its color is blue or black. It represents the focus of energy so that you can obtain a goal. However, you must be in the right place at the right time. Its literal meaning translates to journey. The divinatory meanings of Raidho are limited to change, pilgrimage, journey, quest, progress, destiny, and life lessons. The magical uses of Raidho are limited to ease or bringing about change, to reconnecting and providing protection for travelers. It depicts the path of a person's life and provides detailed information about how it interacts and intersects with other paths. Norse mythology sees these paths as threads of fate, and these paths are solely regulated by the Norns.

Under the first root of the tree, Yggdrasil, there lived three sisters. These women were referred to as the Norns. The Norns tended to the tree using water from the well of Wryd. They play a major role in understanding the mechanism of runic magic and divination. They are responsible for spinning the fates of Gods and men. The threads of fate form a web that consists of complex networks of relationships. Everything that happens in your life is manifested as a thread on the web, and any change in the webbing affects everything else in the system. Most normal people fail to see the web and do most of their actions without being fully aware of its consequences. However, a person who is able to understand the working of this intricate web has a much more solid grasp on things and he or she can control the catalytic reactions following the changes to the web. This makes them masters of their future, as they know exactly what their actions are worth.

This perspective opens a whole new path for the people at Fehu. This revelation helps us to pursue our path with more clarity, which could also help us in benefitting the maximum from its lessons. Without the clarity that it provides, we would end up taking countless detours and constantly find ourselves at dead ends. Raidho does a reality check by reminding us that it may seem like we have achieved all our goals at once, but life and change are consistent and we have to learn to go on with our lives. A person who understands the working of the web will also learn that we are bound to end up where we started, only that we would be in a higher position with a much better perspective. They realize that the journey never really ends. It just progresses from one level to the next.

Kenaz

Kenaz is represented by the sound 'k' and the torch. Its color is yellow. It's a rune of understanding, knowledge, teaching, and learning. It is used in order to view a situation with more clarity than a person normally would. It has been popularized as a beacon or torch in most cases. The divinatory meanings include insight, creativity, wisdom, enlightenment, inspiration, and solution to a problem. The magical uses for Kenaz are fertility, aid in study, creative inspiration source, and also for dispelling anxiety and fear.

As a fun fact, I think I should highlight the fact that the Scottish word "ken" stands for knowing or understanding. It is interesting to note that this is the same way the rune is meant to be interpreted. Inspiration, light and knowledge have always been interpreted as "shedding light on a difficulty" or "bringing a solution to the light." Most of us have seen this depiction in cartoons when we were kids. A light bulb fires up above the head of a person who gets an idea. The same analogy can be used to understand Kenaz. The action of bringing light or its primary purpose is to make the invisible visible. It allows us to take away only bits and pieces of the knowledge we receive. Even that bit of information is provided only at the discretion of the Gods. This surge of knowledge may not be apparent or obvious. In most cases, it may come as a sudden inspiration making a hidden answer suddenly obvious to us.

Scientifically speaking, this kind of information is associated with the right side of our brain. This is due to the fact that it came as a result of opening up your subconscious, rather than through conscious effort. There is also a creative point of view as far as bringing light into darkness is concerned. Another way to look at it would be to see a man carrying a torch and entering into a cave. The fire and air are seen as masculine elements, which join up with the female realm of water and earth. This symbolizes the conception of new ideas due to the joining of male and female counterparts.

Gebo

X

Gebo is represent with the sound 'g' and stands for gift. Its colors are red, silver, and gold. It represents honor and connection created between two people when they exchange gifts. The connection is similar to the connection people have with the gods for giving them life. The divinatory meanings of this rune are relationship, offering, gift, partnership, marriage, love, unexpected good fortune, and generosity. The rune's magical uses extend to finding or strengthening a relationship, to bringing luck. Gebo is specifically a connection rune, specializing in the connection between people. This interesting rune is also responsible for being the one to represent those places where our paths intersect with those of others. It helps us to analyze the true worth of our relationships and decide how to arrive at the best possible outcome. It shows us that relationships are sanctified and strengthened by exchanging gifts between each other.

Wunjo

ᚹ

Wunjo is represented by the sound 'w' or 'v' and stands for joy. Its colors are blue and pink. It shows the balance between all living things in a chaotic world. It's also a rune of friendship, common goals, and wellbeing. If you find this rune in a reading, you can expect good news to follow. The divinatory meanings of Wunjo extend to recognition of achievements, success, bliss, reward, achievement of goals, and contentment. Wunjo can also be a trump card, as it has quite a few useful magical uses. It can be used to motivate a team, to see a task through to full completion, and to achieve success in any endeavor. It is also the patron rune for successfully completing a task.

Coincidentally, Wunjo is the last rune in the first aett. This positioning makes it the rune that represents the end of one cycle. It also prepares you for the beginning of the next cycle, yet another place where people get stalled during their journey. It is a very stable and positive rune... This rune has seen some Christian praise as the poets have made it seem like heaven. However, this hypothesis may not be entirely true, as fact dictates that it resembles the Valhalla. The reason behind this assumption is the belief that this paradise isn't permanent. The glory of Wunjo and the wealth of Fehu have one thing in common. They are both only an illusion. It makes us realize that our success has been limited so far to one level only and that there are many more lessons to be learnt. In spite of all its shortcomings, it serves as a halt where we are given the opportunity to rest, reflect about our journey, and prepare ourselves for the journey that lies ahead. It also offers a new viewpoint, allowing us to look at the journey thus far from a whole new angle.

Hagalaz

ᚺ

Hagalaz is represented by the sound 'h' and stands for hailstone or hail. Its colors are white or blue. It signifies a time or situation of constriction. However, it will eventually turn to water and will flow smoothly. These situations and times will be smooth for us eventually. The divinatory meanings of Hagalaz are destruction, ordeal, sudden loss, testing, clearance, disaster, drastic change, and Karmic lesson. The magical uses of this rune are limited to destroying destructive patterns and to eliminating unwanted influences. The foundation to completely understanding this rune has been laid out by the Norse myth of Ragnarok. This myth encourages us to understand that the annihilation of the old is essential for the growth of the new.

Another interesting fact about Hagalaz is that it lies between sowula (fire) and isa (ice). It reminds us of the Nordic creation myth and the creative potential that exists between these two elements. This is a myth whose interpretation is usually seen from a destructive perspective. This rune shares a similarity with the tower of Tarot; it shares the potential to be viewed in a negative manner. However, this will happen only if we make the choice to see it that way. Viewing this rune in a negative manner deprives us of the opportunity to learn the life lessons it has to offer. Its appearance at the starting of the second aett denotes a new beginning. At the same time, it also hits the serenity and complacency of Wunjo straight out of the park.

Simplifying things, this rune makes sure that, no matter how well things seem to be going for us, we always have to expect a good, old-fashioned whack in the head from the Fates. This is done to make sure that we stay grounded and do not float away with our fantasies and temporary goodwill. The gods will constantly make sure that you stay grounded with such well-timed wake up calls. These kinds of calls will happen very frequently in a person's life. In most cases, these reality checks are seen as repentance for some imagined and nonexistent sin, while in reality they are only reminders about our way of life. They make us focus our attention on the fact that there is a recurrent pattern in our lives, something that we have been consistently overlooking so far. If the intended lesson is not learned for the first time, then these events will keep repeating themselves with increased vigor until the point is made. For an example, let us take the relationship of a person who is dependent on other people. When it comes to breaking off this dependency and, subsequently, the relationship. These people become blindsided. They will engage themselves with such people repeatedly, with more disastrous results each time. This will keep going on until they recognize their flaws and make changes accordingly.

Naudhiz

ᚾ

Naudhiz is represented by the sound 'n' and stands for need or necessity. Its colors are blue or black. It represents how we need or want something that might put a restriction on us. But while it restricts our possibilities, it also contains the power you need to break free of those restrictions. The divinatory meanings of this rune are limited to responsibility, hardship, poverty, obstacle, discontent, and frustration. This rune can also be used for quite a few magical purposes. It is used to represent a need to be filled. In real life, it acts a gentle reminder that is used to let you know that all is not as it should be. To most of us, life appears to be completely out of sync and nothing ever seems to go our way. Regardless of how much you already have, there will always be a silent yearning for more within you. This flaw is only human. The silver lining is that this disapproval with the status quo can be channeled away from the relative safety of Wunjo. It can also be used to motivate them towards change.

Some scholars also state that this rune portrays a balance between a person's assets and desires. The real test lies in how you resolve the situation at hand. The solution will definitely decide the course of the journey. An awareness about the imbalance can also be a very enlightening experience. This causes you to closely watch and assess the worth of your priorities and values. This forces you back onto the path of happiness by default. Naudhiz keeps us in check and will constantly remind us every time we stray from the path.

Isa

|

Isa is represented by the sounds 'I' and 'ee' and stands for ice. Its colors are black and brown. Isa is like the icicle of winter, and when the sun comes along it will melt us from our constricting form and allow us to be free. It signifies a stop in activity until a change occurs. The divinatory meanings of Isa are spread out over blockage, inactivity, potential, stagnation, reflection, patience, withdrawal, standstill, and rest. The magical uses of this rune are limited to representing a primal form and to stopping a process. The myths and deities associated with this rune are Auoumla and Nifelheim.

As people living in modern times, all of us are aware of the representation which shows that fire is usually masculine and earth or ice is feminine. At this point we are not sure if the Norse shared this idea. As far as they were concerned, ice was something that made life difficult for them; it proved to be a huge threat to their navy and their agriculture. However, even they could not ignore the fact that ice was also the beginning of all things. It is very commendable that the Norse people were able to understand the actual role of something so destructive in nature. They believed that fire, although warm and welcome, had no worth unless it is balanced by ice.

This analogy can be extended to the value of life. Life is valued so much because all of us know that death is imminent. Even in our daily lives we require the small death of sleep to be able to be fully functional, physically and emotionally. Isa is a collective rune that contains all of these ideas. The primary representation is a period of rest before any activity. Matter is inert and unreactive by itself, but when united with energy it becomes priceless and worth a lot. It becomes an immovable object that gets acted upon by an unstoppable force.

Jera

Jera is represented by the sounds 'j' and 'y' and stands for the harvest or season. Its color is brown. This rune represents the cycle of life, and with it we see that we have to go with the flow of nature in order to get the goals we want. The divinatory meanings of these runes are reward, cycle turning, change, productivity, motion, and inevitable development. The magical uses of this rune are limited to bringing change, growth, and fertility. In ancient times, the people were more in sync with the various cycles and seasons of the year. They had such a good knowledge of the climates that it is beyond comprehension of the current generation who are only capable of getting used to living in centralized air conditioning.

The ancient people paid so much attention to the weather that it affected their daily activities and even their diet. The whole concept behind this practice was constant change. The whole point of the struggle was to make sure that the people understood the importance of embracing change, rather than standing up against it. It always makes better sense to adjust yourself to a new lifestyle rather than remaining stubborn about sticking to old ways of life. A great farmer would not need a calendar or season guide to tell him when the best time for planting seeds is. Such a person would know the change of seasons like the back of his hand. He would know the exact time to sow seeds and he would be able to accurately predict the patterns of snowing or droughts. The cycle of seasons was a part and parcel of his existence and his whole profession revolved around his prowess to adapt to the change around him.

Jera tends to tail Isa just like spring is followed by winter. The stagnancy of the ice is shattered by the wheel that turns. We have successfully broken through the whole set of "negative" runes in this aett. This achievement did not come from resisting or fighting against the ever hardening ice. It came from experience and the wisdom to wait until the ice thawed enough to make it work. It acts as a much needed catalyst, bringing together everything required to make things go successfully. Irrespective of the harshness of the weather outside, the sun will always come up. So instead of waiting for every storm to blow over, make the most of the present. Enjoy every moment of your life.

Eihwaz

ᛇ

Eihwax is represented by the sounds 'eo' and 'ae' and stands for the yew tree. Its colors are green and white. It is a rune that is used as a magical facilitator and protector. It will show you that, in the event of an ending event, you will find the beginning of a new one. The magical uses of this rune include easing a major life event transition and bringing around profound change. The divinatory meanings of this rune are initiation, change, death, turning point, confrontation of fears, and transformation.

In Northern and Western Europe, the yew tree has had significant importance over the ages. It has been consistently associated with magic, death and runes in those provinces. The main reason behind this analogy with the yew tree is due to its evergreen nature. The yew tree manages to stay green even through the dead time of winter. Furthermore, the red berries of the yew tree are considered to be similar to the blood of life. The yew is regarded to be immortal due to its extremely long life. The yew tree commanded respect as early as the times of the Celts. Even to this day, they are seen in prominent light in the Christian circle.

This rune is the thirteenth rune in the fubark. This marks it in the middle of the alphabet. Along the same lines it may be an interesting coincidence that the death card also holds the number thirteen slots in the Tarot. This rune has a pivotal point in the journey of runes. Every single rite of passage, especially the ones that mark the transition into adulthood, has a symbolism of death. The concept here is that a person's old self has died and has been replaced by a new one. Eihwax is merely a passage through which all of us must pass through at some point of time. This passage guides us through the realm of Hel so that we can gain knowledge about our own mortality. The dark lady of the dead will also be able to open our eyes towards certain mysteries, which can be learned only from her exclusively. The whole prospect is very scary on the outside, but it is something important that we must all go through if we intend to confront our deepest fears and surface with the kind of wisdom that has to be experienced and not taught. Eihwaz is the doorway to this kind of wisdom and it lies between life and rebirth.

Perdhro

Perdhro is represented by the sound 'p' and stands for dice cup. Its colors are red and blue. It reminds you that there are uncertainties in life and stands for freewill, as well as the connections you have to the restrictions you harbor due to your circumstances. It is the rune of memory and problem solving. This rune is represented by the vulva. Its divinatory meanings are magic, mystery, rebirth, sexuality, fertility, divination, prophecy, new beginning, something secret and hidden. The magical uses of this rune are aiding in magic and divination, easing childbirth, fertility, and enhancing psychic abilities.

The way the rune was actually interpreted was very controversial. The main reason behind such accusations was the fact that the P sound does not occur anywhere else in the Germanic alphabet. This raised questions about the authenticity of the word and led to the belief that it was imported from an entirely different language. On top of it all, the old English poem seemed to indicate that it was somehow related to some game. This caused most people to misread it as dice cup or chess pawn. The dice cup interpretation is a fitting match as not only does it look like a vessel for the other runes, it also fits right into the shape of the rune.

Another interpretation of the word comes from the Slavic word "pizda". This meant vulva. When viewed as a symbol of the womb of the goddess, this element has a mysterious and hidden facet to it. However, when taken literally, it is capable of providing a powerful, feminine, sexual counterpart to uruz, thus filling up that space in the fubark. In spite of all the different interpretations, the basic and most widely accepted one is that of a vessel, nurturing and capable of giving birth. It is also capable of keeping all those secrets and mysteries, which make sense only after we embark on the journey that is death. This rune has also seen close association with fate. It believes that the road along which we travel, regardless of whatever choice we make along the way has already been decided when we were born. The simple action of being born into this world has set us on a course of cause and effect where the most insignificant of actions can have an avalanche effect. All of our actions and reactions may be based on the choices we make consciously or through the choices we make unknowingly. Sometimes these choices may even be made as a result of following a particular religious path. All of these actions are done with the hope that we may understand the workings of the world better and see them in a new light.

Elhaz

ᛉ

Elhaz is represented by the sound 'zz' and stands for protection or the elk. Its colors are purple and black. It is a rune of great restraint power, protection, and defense. You should use it in order to protect yourself and your property in the form of charms and talismans. This rune's divinatory meanings are assistance, protection, warning, defense, a mentor, support, and ethical dilemma. Its main magical use is for protection. In Norse mythology, Heimdall is an interesting and mysterious figure. He is always associated with this rune because of his role as guardian and protector. His role is to watch the gate and keep guard over the boundaries between the worlds. He is in charge of all the entering and leaving.

From the perspective of a journey, we have already passed through death and rebirth. Now it is about time that we faced the guardian before we return to our world. Heimdall is the one who charges us to use our newfound power with caution. Such people should no longer think only about themselves; rather, they should also seriously consider how their actions may have a consequence on the others. At this junction, a person may choose to adopt his newfound ethics or ignore the effect it might have on others and constantly focus only on working to their own ends. The bottom line is that the people have been given the sword, which is free to be used at their discretion. It only matters how they decide to put it to use between defense and offence.

Sowulo

ᛋ

Sowulo is represented by the sound 's' and stands for sun. Its color is yellow. By using this rune, you will be able to see things in a clearer picture and, as the sun sheds light on dark times, you will be able to find the light during the dark times. The divinatory meanings for this rune are positive energy, success, power, increase, fertility, activity, and health. The magical uses are strength, energy, healing, success, and fertility. The sun is something that is held in great reverence by almost all the religions that exist in the world. The sun's warmth and light send out a positive vibe. It symbolizes all that is good and flourishing.

The Norse cosmology has an interesting take on the sun's existence. Their records state that the sun is being driven across the cosmos in a chariot. This chariot is chased by a great wolf. This wolf finally gets to devour the sun at Ragnarok. The paganism that has Indo-European roots is always hinting at associating the sun with the horse. They often describe the sun as being carried around the heavens on a horse. Both of these explanations symbolize the same things like fertility and life. The sun is considered masculine in most texts. It is worth it to note that the Norse mythology has the chariot being driven by a girl. The sun wheel, or the swastika, is a very popular motif and it has made frequent appearances in a lot of rock carvings, some dating back to the Neolithic times. They appear pretty frequently across Asia and Europe. The sun rune can also be interpreted as a symbol for energy and motion.

Teiwaz

↑

Teiwaz is represented by the sound 't' and stands for creator. Its colors are red and green. It is a promise of success in your actions, but without personal sacrifice. It also means success in legal problems, but only if you are in the right to begin with. We all know that the second aett began with the cleansing destruction of Hagalaz. The third aett has a similar trait as it begins with a loss as well. The only difference is that this time the loss is more of a choice than an inevitable incident.

Teiwaz relates more to someone who sacrifices something while fully aware of everything that he stands to lose. It is a voluntary sacrifice that is made keeping in mind exactly everything that the person wanted to achieve. It is done with a purpose, and is not the result of a mishap or miscalculation. The divinatory meanings for this rune are discipline, conflict, self-sacrifice, responsibility, strength, duty, physicality, wound, and the warrior path. The magical uses of this rune are limited to protection, strength, and victory, strengthening the wound and healing a wound.

In Norse mythology, Tyr made a sacrifice of his own hand to help in the binding of the Ferris wolf. It was a noble and selfless gesture, especially when it came from a pantheon of deities who were not particularly known for their sense of ethical responsibility and duty. Tyr is believed to be one of the most ancient gods. This is based on the fact that a one-handed warrior was depicted on walls during the Bronze Age in Scandinavia. It is also under speculation that his position among the gods may have originally superseded that of Odin. Tyr's rune also holds the privilege of being one the oldest rune from fubark. It has remained unchanged all the while since the Bronze Age carvings. It stands for all the qualities that are associated with God. It stands for strength, heroism, responsibility and duty. It also houses a deeper mystery. It portrays the wounded god. The pain of this rune is used to draw your focus to forcing discipline. This rune stands apart because the sacrifice made this time was made with full consciousness where the person was fully aware of the reasons and repercussions. When you have come thus far, Uruz has already been confronted and bound. We have learnt the lessons that Hagalaz and Teiwaz have had to offer. This is the path that has to be taken by a warrior.

Berkana

ᛒ

Berkana is represented by the sound 'b' and stands for birch tree or twig. Its colors are blue and white. It represents a new beginning and a powerful rebirth. The divinatory meanings are health, fertility, new beginnings, growth, plenty, conception, and clearance. The magical use of this is for healing, making a fresh, clean start, and achieving conception. The fundamental symbol of fertility is the birch tree. This symbolization is very popular even in European folk tales. In those tales, the birch twigs promote prosperity and make conception a possibility. In those days, they were placed above the door of a sweetheart as a tradition on May Day. They were also placed in houses and stables to increase chances of fertility. It was a popular practice to strike young men, women, and cattle to improve their chances at fertility. The boys would be sent out with twigs of the birch tree, intending to beat the bounds of the parish. It was believed to ring in prosperity in the coming year.

It is interesting to note that witches are often depicted riding birch brooms. This could be because there used to be rituals where people would jump around in the fields with a broom between their legs. The height to which each individual person jumped was supposed to be the exact height to which the crops were supposed to grow. If we consider Teiwaz to be a fundamental male mystery, then Berkana is its counter act. It represents the path of the mother, midwife, and the healer. It is responsible for providing new life just after death, in the same way as the birch tree sheds its leaves at the first sign of the coming winter. While Tyr's wound is a result of a fight or a war or some physical conflict, the wounds of Berkana are those caused by menstruation. Their biggest dilemma now is childbirth. The birch stands for providing, healing through nourishment, empathy, and cleansing.

Ehwaz

ᛖ

Ehwaz is represented by the sound 'e' and stands for horse. Its colors are white and red. It is a reminder that in order to be successful, there has to be a natural flow in the task you are performing. With power and good intentions, you will surely achieve success. The divinatory meanings of this rune are motion, transportation, energy, assistance, communication, power, recklessness, and will. The magical uses of this rune are aiding in communication, power, to send a spell, and transportation. Horses are swift, loyal and strong, for this reason they are considered to be a powerful symbol in many cultures. Their relationships with humans are something very special. It is because of them that we were able to do a lot of things that we would not have been able to do otherwise. We were able to traverse great distance once we had horses at our disposal. The horse is one of very few animals that have managed to retain their power even after being domesticated.

This rune stands for motion and energy. So, we should also pay attention to the source of this energy. It is not a dumb machine that runs on fuel. It is a living, breathing thing that has desires and needs. These needs and desires must be taken into serious consideration instead of just using them as a slave. This rune jolts us into reality and tries to invoke the humanitarian in us. It is trying to show us to use them for help and not as slaves. We could use them for progress, but never to inflict any harm. The horse is like a double-edged sword. It can be a powerful weapon when you want it to be. It can also be a very helpful tool when used in the right way. If left unchecked, you could end up harming yourself as well as those around you. It is a very tempting option to just go ahead wild and recklessly. This would mean that we stand to risk losing that power forever. This is the balance that we must strike to go down the path of pure magic.

Mannaz

ᛗ

Mannaz is represented by the sound 'm' and stands for man (human, not gender). Its colors are purple and blue. It is a rune that allows you to know you can achieve your fullest potential. It also reminds you that all humans share in the experiences of life. And finally, you can use the power of this rune in order to obtain the upper hand in an argument or dispute. Looking at this rune from a broad perspective, one could relate it to represent all of humanity. This reference also encloses the entire realm of Midgard. If you decide to look at the whole thing more specifically, then you will understand that it is meant to point us towards our more personal connections. It makes us aware of our links with our immediate circle of family and close friends, among other people that we care for. It reminds us of the fact that we are social animals. This rune helps us in controlling our social conscience by using the raw energy from Ehwaz. This makes us realize that our actions affect both our magical and mundane deeds.

The divinatory meanings of this rune are family, self, significator, relationships, community, and social concerns. The magical uses of this rune include representing a specific person or a group of people and also establishing strong social relationships. This rune shows the entire web of human relationships. This web has the person or his self at the center.

This is a stark contrast to the web of fate that was explored through the Raidho. The main difference between both these webs is that one is completely fixed while the other is alive, mutable, and constantly changing. This is the place where all the opposites come together, past and present, female and male, and many more. All the opposites are joined and made whole. Mannaz is considered our home. We have been given gifts by the runes. Mannaz speaks for all the lives that we touch through the gifts that we have been given.

Laguz

ᛚ

Laguz is represented by the sound 'l' as in lake and stands for lake or water. Its colors are green, white, and black. It represents the power of water and the flowing of nature. It is letting you know that you must go with the flow and to take full advantage of your power. The divinatory meanings of this rune are fears, emotions, hidden things, unconscious mind, intuition, revelation, and counseling. The magical uses of this rune help you to confront fears, enhance psychic abilities, stabilize emotional or mental disorders, and uncover hidden things. The emotions that most people see when they look at water are love, peacefulness, intuition, compassion, and emotions in general. We should remember that water to the Norse was not the same as we see it. For them, water was associated with the sea. The sea was a grave place for them. It was terrifying and unforgiving. It was unpredictable for them. On top of all that, it also housed the Midard serpent in its waters. The sea was also a watery grave for many sailors who had traversed across its surface.

This rune has to be seen as both the light and dark sides of the element of water. It relates to all our primal fears, like darkness, the cold, and other terrifying things hidden deep within out subconscious. This rune makes us aware of our darkest fears and threatens to make it all a reality. There are many factors that hinder our spiritual progress; laguz makes us see the whole thing in a whole new light and gives us the opportunity to modify those aspects that keep pulling us down. It also gives us the opportunity to examine the most underlying details with great scrutiny. In this aspect, this rune is very similar to Eihwaz. The experience, understanding, and wisdom garnered by the other runes and Eihwaz has made us ready and prepped to see that dark side for what it really is. It makes us accept the dark side as an integral part of our self. This rune also brings men up to the task of helping other people through this self-examination process. This allows them to empathize more strongly and share their own experiences without any barriers. This approach makes it the unspoken rune of the spiritual counselor.

Inguz

ᛝ

Inguz is represented by the sound 'ng' such as in 'long' and stands for fertility. Its colors are black and brown. It is a protective rune that is used in protection of homes for the most part. In order to use this rune effectively, you should learn to build up your powers over time and release the power all at once. The divinatory meanings of this rune are productivity, work, groundedness, bounty, connection with the land, and balance. The magical uses are farming, fertility, general health, growth, and balance. Inguz is the God of fertility and agriculture. It is an Anglo-Saxon or Danish name for Freyr. Agriculture is one of man's first successful attempts at controlling the environment around him for his profit and personal gain. Therefore, it is unanimously understood that their concerns would revolve around the consistent fertility of their crops, animals, and people. It has been the most basic concern of almost all the pagan agrarian societies.

From ancient times until modern times, the people have always tried to get the maximum benefit out of the land through the success of their own crops. A large majority of the developed countries in the West have lost the knowhow and skill required to cultivate a bumper crop. In their race for development and modernization, they have forgotten that they used to be sons of the soil once upon a time. The spiritual consequences that arose due toman's segregation from the ways of the earth have been particularly disastrous. It has become more and more difficult for the people to relate to a natural deity in an all man-made environment.

The shape of this rune may be misleading, as it could direct you to the fields. However, its real significance lies in representing the harmonious balance that we have developed with the four elements and four directions. It is a reminder of the connection that the gods shared with the earth. It reestablishes our connection with our spiritual natures in a more physical manner. In the literal sense, it is a grounding rune. Its main function is to reconnect us with our roots. It reintroduces us to the earth, reestablishing the connection with our minds and our spirits.

Dagaz

Dagaz is represented by the sound 'd' as in 'day' and stands for day. Its color is yellow. It represents stability between the opposites like light and dark. It is able to stop harmful energy and allows the good energy to get through to you. The divinatory meanings of this rune are success, happiness, activity, satisfaction, and a fulfilling lifestyle. The main magical use of this rune is to bring a positive outcome. This rune marks the end of the third aett. This leaves only the othala rune to finish the cycle. As was the trend in the last two aetts this aett ends with hope and light. Wunjo is used to represent the sun and earthly glories. The day brings more abstract light and power of Sowulo. This power is brought down to earth and it is applied into our daily lives. The shape of the rune is itself a dead giveaway of the interconnection it represents. It reminds us most about Gebo. This is because of its balance of the feminine and masculine and with the four elements.

There are other runes that make a connection with the natural and celestial realms as well. It is very similar to Inguz, as it symbolizes harmony with one's environment. However, it is not limited to just the physical environment. It also implies a pronounced harmony with the spiritual environment as well. It is a harmony of all the six cardinal points. These cardinal points are the four directions of the compass, the celestial realm of the heavens above us, which houses the gods, and the realm below the heavens. It also includes all the spirits of nature and that of the earth. All these facets are brought together through Dagaz and brought into our daily lives.

Othala

Othala is represented by the sound 'o' as in 'old' and stands for home or ancestral land. Its color is brown or copper. It is the rune of wealth, but it represents a wealth that is unable to be sold. It's the wealthy like family or friends. It also represents enclosure and how things currently exist. The divinatory meanings are land, property, home, inheritance, legacy, permanence, synthesis, and sense of belonging. The magical uses include help in completing a project, acquiring property or land, and, strengthening family ties. In othala we find ourselves back in the mundane and meaningless world of property and wealth among other riches. In this facet this rune is very similar to what Fehu stands for. Cattle and other animals are a more movable or transitory form of wealth that may or may not last for a very long time. However, a property of land is immovable and lasts for a very long time. Land can be passed down as a legacy. More importantly, land defines us for the person we are. It ultimately becomes our home.

This rune brings us to the seventh cardinal point. The seventh cardinal point is the center. It is the place where Midgard and Asgard meet. It is like a meeting point between the gods and us. It is the axis around which our lives revolve. The idea of owning land or any property is only a symbolization that should help us find our centers. All of us have our own centers, which each of us should find in order to give more meaning to our lives. It is the ultimate goal of the runic journey. Eventually, all of us discover the truth that, in spite of all the traveling we do, in the end, all of us just go home. This does not necessarily mean that all of our travels have been in vain. It is only through such exploration that our home or spiritual center can have any meaning to us. The word *home* will have no meaning unless and until we fully understand what our home is to us. All the lessons that we learned throughout our lives will have absolutely no effect if we don't find a way to integrate them into our daily lives. This rune not only concludes the third aett, but it also brings around the cycle of the fubark itself. From this point we have to begin the grand journey of the runes again.

Chapter 4
Uses

Runes first started out as a form of writing and, to this day, still have a strong set of roots in the world in terms of communication. Since you are reading this now, it is very likely that you are already familiar with at least the concept of runes. Don't worry, you are not alone: As we have mentioned in previous chapters, runes, rune writing and the runic language Havre both fascinated and captured the imaginations of people since their original inception thousands of years ago. Runes were at first considered a secret language known only to the wisest and most esoteric of individuals, such as shamans, wandering sages, or particularly celebrated god kings the likes of Odin the All-Father, patron god of Nordic mythology.

Ancient cultures over the centuries of human civilization have used runes to empower amulets, jewelry, and weapons borne by warriors into battle, which in turn were believed to bestow magical powers of protection or other enchantments on those who wore them. Some warriors, such as the legendary berserkers, are believed to have tattooed runes all over their body, believing that the signs would grant them great strength and make them invulnerable to sword cuts and arrow strikes. Runes have been carved on graves and massive standing stones, both to commemorate a great person or celebrate an achievement, as well as to help guide the spirit to the afterlife. Runes have been spoken and sung as part of magical incantations, and of course, cast in the form of runestones believed to hold the power to divine the future. In fact, even the Nazis that rose to power in Germany in the years leading up to World War II were purportedly fascinated by runes and the supernatural powers that one could glean from knowing their meanings.

Even in the modern day, we see renditions of runes in popular culture, especially in fantasy novels and movies such as *Lord of the Rings* and the *Harry Potter* series, and even in video games like *The Elder Scrolls: Skyrim*. One interesting observation one could make about all these instances is that runes are almost always associated with some sort of mystical significance. Even in the stories and fantasy fiction we tell today, we like to attribute at least a small degree of underlying magical power in these cryptic symbols from civilization's storied past. Whether they contain actual magic, are used as symbols and charms, or contain the power to foretell the future or tap into the distant past, runes have never failed to captivate the minds of its readers.

Unfortunately, one obvious downside to this enduring

popularity is that a great deal of confusion and misinformation, honest or deliberate, has cropped up about runes. As a result of this sad happenstance, a great deal of popular assumptions about the nature, the significance, and possible uses of runes, have been rendered inaccurate, distorted by time and historical events. As well, the meaning behind some symbols—for example, the infamous swastika—is now almost universally and instinctively perceived as a sign representing absolute evil and human cruelty, which is a far cry from its original meaning.

In Germanic runology, various runes represented a certain letter in the alphabet, and these also were used in representing whole words. 'Whole words' are mentioned here because an important tool in understanding how runes are perceived lies in language itself. As our understanding of language has evolved over time, so has our understanding of runes. As the years passed these went from being a form of writing to having a lot other meanings and uses, which we will discuss in greater detail in this chapter.

Another of these meanings that will be dealt with in greater detail in the next chapter is that of using runes to foretell possible events in a person's life. For centuries, people have used runes to look at the path that a person is on and to use these to direct them and advise them. A lot of information can be gained from a rune if you know the things that you need to be looking for and if you know the meanings behind each of the runes that you have. This is by no means a way to tell a person's fortune, but it is a way that you can guide them towards certain life events that they will undertake that can lead to a certain outcome. If the person does not like the outcome that they are looking at, then they can always alter their life to make the needed changes to their present course.

Runes can also be used in another way of helping to communicate with those that have passed on. While this is a very difficult and controversial thing to do, there are those that will generally say that you need to be careful when doing this, as it is not something that you need to try and do on your own. You need to make sure that you talk to a rune caster before you try this type of procedure as this can lead to some issues or, in most cases, will not lead to anything at all if you are not experienced enough in the use of runes. I heard of a person that tried this one time and did not have the best of experiences when doing this. They had heard that runes might be useable in talking with a loved one that had recently passed. They even went to a rune caster and they were not able to make the connections to the loved one that had died. This is usually the result of these types of inquiries.

In closing, runes have a load of power that they can offer a person in terms of learning a new language, having a better understanding of aspects of their life, or, in rare cases, being able to communicate with a loved one that you never got to say goodbye to. In all, runes will make an impact in your life and are very much something that you will want to make sure that you learn all that you can about to get a better understanding of.

Chapter 5
Runes And Magic

Runes and magic is a very confusing title, as this can, to a large degree, be very misleading and give a person the wrong impression about the true benefits of runes. This chapter is designed to help and sort out some of the facts from a lot of the myths that are associated with runes. At the end of this chapter, you will hopefully have a lot better understanding of how these work and what the connection they have to magic really is.

Earlier in the book we discussed the origins and history of runes. Since their earliest forms, runes have been deeply and closely connected with magic. As we have seen, the *Havamal* epic poem in Nordic mythology gives us an account of how wise Odin sought to understand runes and their power to bring the dead back to life. The Nordic sagas and epic poems also make many references to oracles and rune readers capable of using runes to divine the future. Runes have been carved onto the staffs used by tribal shaman in rituals and etched onto immense standing runestones that still can be found in their original locations in Scandinavia today.

We also talked a little about the uses of runes in terms of dealing with a person's fortune. This belief has ancient roots that grow deep into the soil of human history, probably far deeper than even modern day historians are capable of unearthing. While it has proven difficult for linguists of our day and age to find specific references in ancient Nordic texts that contain specific "How To" instructions on using runes to foretell the future, the use of runes to divine portents and omens of upcoming events is widely mentioned in the many examples of literature pertaining to Norse mythology. For instance, Tacitus's *Germania*, written sometime in the 1st Century; Rimbert's Vita *Ansgari*, written in the 9th century; and Snorri Sturluson's *Ynglinga saga*, written in the 13th century; all contain references that attribute runes or rune-like symbols with the ability to divine the future, if cryptically. In Tacitus's *Germania*, there is mention of "signs" that were chosen in groups of three, and cut into the grains of a "nut bearing tree." In Sturluson's *Ynglinga saga*, King Granmar of Sodermanland travels to Uppsala to attend a ritual that he believes will grant him a vision of his own future. There, "chips" are marked in sacrificial blood, shaken, and cast like dice in front of a rune reader, who relates to the king that the markings on the chips have divined that the king has not long to live. Finally, in Rimbert's *Vita Ansgari*, there are multiple accounts of runes being used in divination. Here, another king, Anund Uppsale, leads a large Danish fleet of warships intending to plunder the trading town of Birka and raze it to the ground.

However, Uppsale has an abrupt change of heart and decides to "consult the Aesir" as to whether or not the attack should be carried out. To commune with the gods, Uppsale called his Danes to "draw lots"—while the exact process is not described, the "lots" that were drawn were apparently quite informative, and the king saw this as a sign that if Birka were attacked, they would suffer dire consequences and extreme bad luck. So, as can be seen, the use of magical runes and symbols to divine the future has a strong precedence in ancient history and folklore.

Keeping these stories in mind, it is very important that we begin this conversation by understanding that runes are not a means of fortune telling and are not set in stone. Often if a person gets a reading from these, they will then say it is set in stone that a certain series of events will transpire in their life. These are instead meant to lay out for the person a series of events that seem to be on their way to happening. This shows the person the path that they are on and the potential outcome that will come from this path.

Another thing that should be looked at closely is that these answers can be very well presented or can actually hide their exact meaning. You will need to at times have the advice and expertise of a rune caster to help you see these answers. Don't despair if the rune caster has some issues in getting your answers, as this is, again, not an exact science that is flawless all the time. Some rune casters will have the answers pop to them, while still others will have to work hard to get the exact answer. This is not a reflection of the person reading the runes but instead a result of the runes themselves, as they can at times be very difficult to read and to get their meaning.

If you are not with the path that the rune says that you are currently on, you will have the power to take measures that will affect the overall outcome of your path. Too many people see these readings and feel that it is too late for them to take action, as they mistakenly feel that this is a set path that cannot be changed. The most basic of moves will help to cancel out the negative reading that has set you on the path that you are currently on. To go back to our previous example, King Anund Uppsale was able to divine that disaster and bad luck would befall his fleet were they to proceed with their plans to attack the city of Birka; by diverting their attack, they were able to avoid the tragedy and misfortune that had been divined.

The word *rune* actually is loosely translated to mystery, secret, or whisper. This is one of the reasons why runes have been so popular in the world of magic. It is also a good idea to know that each rune has its very own property that is associated with it. In the end, these properties are the way that rune casters are able to look at runes and help to guide you through a variety of choices that you will have to make in your life. Each rune also translates to words that, to the people that discovered them, held high value. It is for this reason that you need to know the meanings behind, and all of the variations of runes before you can truly understand and appreciate the full power that runes can have in a person's life. Each of these runes has a story that has been associated with them and in turn are associated with a Norse god for each rune. Again, this is information that you will need to have to fully grasp the significance that these can play in a person's life.

Now that you know about the runes and some of the uses for them, let's talk about how you can use them in your daily life in the magical sense. Runes are actually very simple to use, and that's why most people like to start with them when they dive into the world of magic. They're pretty easy to understand, and casting them for a reading is very easy.

Runes are usually not used to tell the future anymore, but there are many other uses for them, too. But first, you need a set of runes! To begin, you can choose rocks that seem to call to you or pieces of wood. You can then cleanse the rocks in water for a few days, and then let them dry a few more days. Take a permanent marker and carefully write the runes on each stone. You want stones that are somewhat similar in size so they're easier to handle. If you choose to go with wood, you can use sharpie on the pieces of wood or you can burn the symbols using a soldering iron. The material doesn't matter, but the more natural and personal they are to you, the more accurate readings you will get.

You'll need a bag for your runes. Most people like to carry them around in a store bought or homemade silk bag in order to keep them safe, and it makes them a bit more fashionable. However, whatever you store them in doesn't matter.

You can create a ritual for your casting, or you can just cast the runes. If you choose to create a personal ritual, try to make it something that is personal to you. Use your favorite incense and wash your hands with rosewater. It doesn't really matter what you do. Then you'll finally do the casting.

In order to do a casting, you'll want a quiet place where you know you won't be disturbed. You'll then need to empty your mind and free it from everything but the question you want to ask. Then, reach into the bag of runes and pull one out at random. Focus on what you believe it's telling you.

The trick to reading runes is to be sure that you're phrasing the question in a way that can be answered. Runes do not answer *yes* or *no* questions very well, so make sure it's not something like 'Does Henry love me?' or 'Am I going to get that promotion?' Instead, phrase your questions more like 'How can I get that promotion I want?' or 'What will happen if I go out on a date with Henry?'

If you believe that your problem is going to need more than a single-rune answer, then you might want to go for something a little more complex. Picking a handful of runes at random and then placing them onto a piece of square silk will work well. Take into account the positions of the runes. Their reversed meanings are different than their upright positions. Also look at how close they are together, and what order they're in. This will give you a lot more to work with.

You can also try the three-rune method. Just pick three runes from the bag. The first is the problem. The second is the cause. The third is the outcome.

For example, let's say you're having a problem with a coworker and you need to know how to resolve it peacefully. You draw your first rune. It represents communication. So far, you know that you need to talk to that person in an honest manner and communicate with them. The second rune is the cause, and you pull out a rune that means ice. This could represent that you and your coworker are at an impasse, and maybe you've tried to figure out what the problem is but failed. So far, you don't know what to do in order to communicate with your coworker.

The third rune you pull out represents the aggressor. It doesn't mean that you need to become nasty with the coworker, but it might be telling you that you need to take a more direct, bold approach to the problem. Perhaps it's telling you to arrange a meeting with this coworker to tell them why you're not happy and explain how his or her actions are hurting you.

Now, this may seem a little straightforward to you, but that's the point of runes! They're there to tell you the things that may seem obvious to others but are not obvious to you. They are meant to open your eyes to the world around you and make you think harder about what actions you are or are not taking. The more thought you give to the runes, the more useful answers you will get back.

You should remember to never expect an easy solution when it comes to magic. It's about hard work and inspiration. The runes are not meant to think for you, but to help you think for yourself.

Chapter 6
Celtic History

Can runes also help us unravel the mysteries and understand the history of an entire people? Yes, they can—as we will see in this chapter, runes and the meaning of language inscribed therein are pivotal tools that we can use to understand the Celts.

But just who were the Celts? The first known recorded use of the name 'Celts,' rendered in Greek as Keltoi, is attributed to the Greek geographer Hecataeus of Miletus, who wrote about a people living near Massilia, a region that corresponds to what is now the modern day city of Marseille, France. Herodotus, another famous Greek scholar and philosopher, also makes reference to the Keltoi living around the Danube and also somewhere in the wild, far western reaches of Europe. Etymologically speaking, linguist Partizia De Bernado Stempel suggests that the term keltoi means "the tall ones," in reference to the people of the region being particularly tall compared to the ancient Greeks who lived during that same period in history.

In a few centuries, however, we see that the use of term Keltoi itself becomes muddled. By the 1st century BC, Julius Caesar makes reference that the people the Romans knew as Gauls had, in fact, called themselves Celts. This would imply that even if it was the Greeks that first started calling these tribes the Keltoi, somehow the name stuck and became widespread enough that the Celts adopted it for their own use to refer to the collective tribes of Gaul, tribes which were spread out over a more expansive area than the Keltoi people, who had once restricted their settlement to the Massilia region. Later scholars in the Roman period would only dilute the specificity of the term further: Strabo. The geographer, refers to the same people as both Gallic and Celtic, and Pliny the Elder uses various forms of 'Celt' or 'Celtici' as a sort of clan surname for individual families or tribal clans, further complicating the use of the term.

In modern day academic circles, the term 'Celts' refers to the people who lived in Medieval Europe during the Iron Age, who spoke Celtic languages and had many cultural similarities. Unfortunately, that is where the certainty in scholarship ends. Of continuing controversy and increasing debate is how closely these cultural groups are related, or if they should even be linked at all in terms of ethnicity, linguistic tendencies, and cultural practices. Even the exact geography that constitutes the borders of the ancient Celtic territory is under dispute. Of particular concern to modern day historians is whether or not to consider the Iron Age inhabitants of Great Britain and Ireland as part of the greater Celtic culture.

An important tie that scholars can use to describe the unified Celtic people as a whole is the language they shared. There is a tenuous academic consensus that the earliest direct example of a unified Celtic language is the Lepontic runes, or inscriptions that first surfaced in the 6th century BC. It is important to note that very little of this language remains; what we know of it today, we know exclusively from inscriptions and the names of places.

Indeed, their runic inscriptions and language are key to understanding the Celtic peoples as a unified whole. In modern times, the word 'Celtic' refers not just to the people, but to the family of languages they shared in common. Language is the key element that links the disparate ancestral tribal cultures together, and it is the written form of this language—in the form of runic inscriptions—that links artifacts with their significance to the culture. We will see that it is language that reveals the modern notion of a uniquely characterized, fleshed out, and identifiable Celtic cultural identity, defined by shared similarities among languages, classical texts, works of art, tangible historic artifacts, and even social organization and mythology. Some historians go so far as to claim that the Celtic people have more of a cultural and linguistic heritage than a genetic one. As we have discussed, Celtic cultures might have had massively diverse places of origin and cultural customs, but the one thing they had in common was the use of a common set of Celtic languages, both written and oral.

As far as modern day historians have discovered, the earliest known speakers of a unified set of Celtic languages emerged around 400 BC. During this time, the tribes had already split into various language groups and were spread out across the rugged plains and rolling hills of Western continental Europe, the Iberian Peninsula, Britain, and Ireland.

If a single culture must be chosen as an origin point for the Celts as a distinct cultural branch, some scholars have nominated the Urnfield people of western Middle Europe. Thriving sometime circa 1300 BCE - 750 BCE, the Urnfield culture left behind linguistic evidence to suggest that they spoke Proto-Celtic, a language recently believed to have been the ancestor of all later Celtic languages. The Urnfield tribes got their name from their custom of cremating the dead and interring their ashes in urns, which were then buried in the grassy fields of their homeland. During the late Bronze Age, the Urnfield culture saw a dramatic rise in population, likely due to discoveries in agriculture and technology that marked the advancement of civilization into the Iron Age. It has been suggested by the Greek historian Ephorus of Cyme, writing in the 4th century BC, that the Celts of this region were driven from their ancestral homeland by frequent wars and "the violent rising of the sea." And as the Urnfield people spread further and further outward from their ancient homeland and split into distinct cultural groups, they brought with them not only their tools and technology, but also their languages.

The Celtic cultures that emerged in Iron Age Europe from the eighth century BCE brought about ground-breaking consequences, not the least of which was the hasty downfall of the prehistoric societal system, which can be traced back far into the Stone Age. With the usage of a raw material that could be shaped into tools, weapons and ornaments that was accessible to everyone, there was great power—both politically and socially-- to be taken.

From around 500 BCE, the trade routes within the Mediterranean world began to increase, with more contacts emerging. At the same time, the Scythian horsemen from the Siberian and Russian steppes pushed westward and had a substantial role in art, clothing, oral literature, and military strategies throughout central Europe. In the Hallstatt culture, which is located in modern day Austria, there was a fusion of cultural stimuli from the Scythians, the Etruscans, and the Greeks, which gave rise to the Celtic customs that would spread across Europe.

It was the Hallstatt cultures that directly succeeded the Urnfield people by the early 1st millennium BC. With their farmers equipped with iron tools and their warriors with iron weapons, the Hallstatt cultures did well for themselves during the early

Iron Age. And it was the Hallstatt cultures that are credited for spreading the use of early Celtic languages to Iberia, Ireland, and Britain. Interestingly, some scholars see Celtic languages as the earliest indicator of the rise of the Celtic people. After all, we know that the Celtic languages had been flourishing long, long before any evidence of a distinct Celtic culture can be found through archeology.

Whilst the Mediterranean world and a significant portion of western and central mainland Europe emerged from the prehistoric era and stepped into historic times, the Germanic cultures in the northern areas of Europe were still to experience roughly another 1500 years of unwritten prehistory. However, the relationships between the 'civilized' Mediterranean world and the Germanic world would continue to have a great impact on each other, politically, socially, and religiously.

In order to understand these radical changes and the following rise of the Celtic power, we must first understand the relationship between the cultural phases—the Late Bronze Age and the Hallstatt and La Tene periods—and additionally, the relationship with the Mediterranean region.

In northern Europe, where the Celtic cultures would emerge, the Bronze Age societies were marked by a high degree of consistency. This can be seen with the ruling classes in particular. In particular, the burial practices began to change in the Germanic cultures—at this time, the bodies of the deceased were cremated and the ashes placed in clay urns and positioned in grave fields, which would give the society its name of the Urnfield culture. The Urnfield culture was named after a site in Austria which flourished around 1200 – 800 BCE and shows its importance with the establishment of ironwork.

At this time, the relationship with the Mediterranean world began to forge stronger links. The ruling elite built strong, reinforced communities strategically positioned on top of hilltops. The society was ruled over by a single leader who would offer his strength and safety in exchange for control over luxury and everyday goods needed. We can see this yearning for luxury goods and status in finds of rich caches and sacrificial offerings uncovered from many archaeological excavations.

Between 800 – 600 BCE, there were several important changes that took place. In the region from modern day France to the Czech Republic and all the way to the Balkans, inhumation began to be the initial method of burial practice. At this time, there were numerous rich, princely inhumations (known as Furstengraber) that took place amongst the ruling, elite classes. These were typically made up of wooden chambers containing four wheeled carts, horse paraphernalia, and luxury grave goods. We can see this same practice far to the South Russian steppes in the Timber Grave culture, although it is not known for certain whether it was here that the practice originated. What it does highlight, however, is the emergence of a powerful warrior aristocracy in Europe. It is probable that there was no one political power ruling over everyone, but instead it is likely that there were numerous tribes which were constantly at war with each other and were led by their particular chiefs. During this period, however, the relationship with the Mediterranean world had come to a complete standstill.

It was, without a doubt, the transition from bronze to iron, along with all the various deep-rooted changes that came about with the material, which was the cause for these changes.

From 600 BCE, there were significant political changes that took place, and contacts with the Mediterranean world began to develop once more. Greek colonization reached its peak from 750 – 550 BCE, with the Greek culture spreading towards Italy and southern France, places where it had significant impact on the local cultures. Greece experienced its Classical Age around 500 BCE and then, in a few centuries, the Roman Empire would emerge onto the scene, an occasion which would have dramatic consequences throughout Europe.

The relationships between the cultures both north and south of the Alps can be seen in the importation of the beautiful luxury goods that date from around this time. Not only did they import these stunning goods to showcase their power and status, but the people of these cultures were able to refine their own individual artistic and technical skills. At the settlement of Heuneburg in modern day Germany, the individual who designed it based it on styles from the Mediterranean. We see this in other settlements including Hohenasperg and Breisach in Germany, andMont Lassois in France; these show that feudal society had begun in Europe.

These sites also illustrated the point that feudal Europe ceased during the sixth century BCE, in what is known as the last phase of the Hallstatt era. Archaeologists have not discovered any evidence to prove that these chiefdoms managed to continue during the La Tene era. In the fifth century BCE, Europe underwent massive changes—princely burials became popular throughout, and placed with them were ritual ornaments known as the early Celtic Le Tene type. The relationship with the south had great influences in the artistic designs of the European cultures, with the old motifs of waterfowl and horses disappearing at the same time. Europe was undergoing its own process of orientalizing; the Celtic culture had begun.

Whilst the Scythian people settled in the eastern steppes, the early Celtic tribes spread out over immense areas from their original homeland along the upper reaches of the River Rhine. We don't know for sure what the reasons were for this expansion—theories of overpopulation and internal struggles have been submitted—but the course of events has been shown through the archaeological sources. Herodotus called these people the 'Keltoi' and said they lived further west than any other people. Eforos, another ancient Greek writer, tells us that the Keltoi were one of four great barbarian cultures which included the Sycthians, Persians, and Libyans. In the Roman period, the Keltoi were known as the Gauls. It was in the eastern reaches of the Gaul territory that the western La Tene culture arose.

During the fifth and sixth centuries BCE, the Celtic culture grew with the rise of various warrior tribes. There was a great trading relationship, with the northern Celtic tribes offering furs, food, gold, iron, furs and slaves, in exchange for luxury goods from the southern Mediterranean civilizations. However, with Greek colonization came Greek ships; these merchant ships were able to reach the trading routes that had once only been reached through Etruscan ports. With the Persian Wars and other political events, the Greeks interest in these areas lessened, and along with the Greek cities in Italy forming an independent region, were the reason for the long-standing Celtic societal disintegration and their expansion over Europe. The Celtic culture never became a singular society or an actual ethnic group. Although the Celtic tribes were distantly related, most tribes spoke different languages. The chiefs of these tribes created numerous independent regions that were administered from *oppida*. These were typically heavily fortified and positioned on hilly ground, but were considered great cultural centers.

Scholars have suggested that there were more than 700 *oppida* in Gaul alone, many of which became recognized in connection with Caesar's campaigns.

The Celtic tribes spread to the Alps as well, and would eventually became the first traditionally recognized tribes of the Alps. Beginning with the Canegrate culture, which is regarded as the first of several migratory waves, the early Celtic tribes made the long, perilous journey through the Alpine passes and settled in force in the western Po valley, claiming vast and verdant territories located between Lake Maggiore and Lake Como. However, some historians have also suggested that an even earlier Celtic culture made the journey across the Alps long before this, during the Middle Bronze Age; Celtic bronze artifacts and ornaments seem to support this claim. The Celtic world became known as a melting pot of various cultures, incorporating various influences from the Greeks, Etruscans, and the Scythians into their own religious, artistic, and social structure.

In time, the Celtic tribes spread out over much of Europe at times through peaceful colonization, other times through brutal wars. In around 400 BCE, Celtic tribes from modern day Switzerland arrived in Italy; they were able to defeat the Roman army at the River Allia in 386 BCE and were able to carry on and sack Rome. They then headed down south towards Sicily. Whilst this was happening, the Celtic tribes were settling in southern Britain, including Cornwall, Wales, and eventually Scotland.

During the third century BCE, other Celtic tribes pushed through into the Balkans but were defeated in 279 BCE. Others headed towards Asia Minor and established the region known as Galatia.

The Celtic tribes in Italy, in particular the Lepontic culture, are of especial importance to scholars of Celtic language, as it was the Lepontic people who spoke the oldest Celtic language since 6th century BCE. And the Lepontic culture had a wide distribution, ranging as far as Switzerland and Northern-Central Italy, spanning the regions from the Alps to Umbria. We know of the Lepontic culture's wide distribution from a wealth of more than 760 Gaulish inscriptions unearthed throughout present day France, which stand as firm testaments to the deep penetration of Celtic heritage and influence within the Italian peninsula.

It is worthwhile to note that the Celtic presence can be felt as far as Iberia as well, specifically, the regions of modern day Spain and Portugal. Interestingly, academics with an interest in Celtic civilization do not strongly acknowledge their presence in Iberia; this has been mostly due to the lack of archeological and linguistic findings. However, modern scholarship in language, art, religion, and newly discovered inscriptions have clearly proven that Celtic influences in Spain and Portugal are indeed prominent, and so significant that they could possibly claim the highest saturation of settlements in Western Europe.

Today, the historic Celtic presence in Iberia is commonly

divided into two main archeological and cultural groups, though the distinction between the two is not very clear. First, the Lustian group, speakers of Proto and Para Celtic languages, settled along Galicia and the Iberian Atlantic coastline, as well as the southwest of the Iberian Peninsula. They shared territories and borders with the Celtici, Vettones, and Vacceani people of central to western Spain and Portugal. The second group of Iberian Celts was the Celtiberian group, who settled in central Spain and the Upper Ebro Valley, and were largely made up of migrant Celts from France and integrated with the local Iberian cultures.

The Celtic world was mainly positioned in what is modern day France, Germany and Italy, and was known as Gallia Narbonensis and Gallia Cisalpinia by the Romans. The former was annexed into the Roman Empire in 121 BCE, although there were many bloody struggles for a long time afterwards. By the time of the first recorded contact between the Romans, the Gauls were a people who mostly spoke Celtic. Interestingly, though the Romans and Gauls fought numerous battles and feuded as longtime rivals over land and territories among their shared borderlands, the Gauls, at least, adopted many Roman innovations and cultural tendencies. For instance, Gaulish cities during the later Iron Age adopted a social organization system that resembled that of the Romans', with large, independently governed towns not unlike that of the city-states of Rome, albeit on a smaller scale. More noticeably, from the 3rd century BC onwards, the Gauls adopted their own form of coinage. Based on a thorough analysis of place names and runic inscriptions on artifacts recovered from this period, historians have suggested that the Gaulish Celtic language was spoken over most of what is now modern day France. The Gauls continued to grow and expand their territories, which consistently conflicted with Roman interests. Sporadic border conflicts eventually culminated in the Gallic Wars of 58-51 BC. Following this conflict, the Celtica of Caesar's day formed the main part of Roman Gaul, renamed as the province of Gallia Lugdunensis. This territory bordered Garonne to the south and the Seine and the Marne farther to the north.

Despite the warlike political dominance of the Celtic people being crushed through the extensive campaigns by Caesar and the expansion of the Roman Empire, the Celts were able to ensure that their religion, art, music and overall culture continued to survive right into present times. We can see this particularly in places such as Brittany, Wales, and Ireland, where the Celtic people were able to flourish for centuries.

Archaeological excavations in Denmark and other northern European countries have unearthed artifacts that originated from Celtic workshops from central Europe and were transported to the northern Celtic people via trade routes. One particular object found was the renowned silver cauldron from

Gundestrup in Vesthimmerland, which was most likely a sacrificial offering to the gods.

The administration developments which were changing in the south had a direct impact on the Celtic tribes to the north in an exchange of goods, but this time it was with the Roman Empire.

Various Roman historians have given us detailed accounts on the many different Celtic tribes and this is the first time we learn of their particular names. In addition to this, we learn about their customs, traditions, religious beliefs and political structures. These Germanic Celtic tribal chiefs were considered to be formidable commanders and this is particularly visible in the accounts penned by Tacitus in his Annales and Germania, along with other writers such as Pliny and Vergil.

These Roman accounts have proven vital to our understanding of Celtic tribal culture. However it is important to note that they are, by nature, limited to the scholarly interests of Rome at the time. We know much about the intricacies of the Celtic mercantile system, their culture, and social hierarchies, for instance, but much else, such as the organization of the Celtic family, has been lost to time simply because these were not subjects of any interest whatsoever to the scholars of Imperial Rome.

However, even in light of these limitations, the importance of these accounts should not be diminished. From these accounts, we now know that the pre-Christian Iron Age Celtic cultures organized themselves into a social order based, foremost, on a formal class structure. At the top of this social order was a king, though there is some mention of an oligarchical or republican forms of government emerging in tribal areas that enjoyed a closer relationship with Roman settlements. Caesar and his contemporary scholars also describe the Gauls as ascribing to a patron and client relationship quite similar to those of Roman society. Tribes that could not field their own military, for instance, might become 'clients' of better armed 'patron' tribes in exchange for agricultural goods, trade crafts, or other services.

Beneath the king, according to these Roman accounts, is a division of three groups: a class of aristocratic warriors; a class of intellectuals such as druids, poets, and jurists, magistrates or other lawgivers and authority figures; and at the bottom was everyone else: farmers, tradesmen, merchants, laborers, and slaves.

And slavery was indeed a practice carried out by the Celts, their system of which likely shared many similarities with the slavery perpetrated in ancient Greece and Rome. Slaves came from a variety of sources. They were prisoners of war, raiding, or were criminals carrying out a penal sentence or debt repayment. Like their Greek and Roman influences, it is possible that slavery among the Celts was hereditary, though it was possible for a slave to earn his or her own freedom. There is evidence that slavery was quite widely practiced within Celtic territories, and was particularly widespread during the Middle Ages. For instance, the Celtic word for "female slave" was used as a general unit of mercantile value: That the word for female slaves would be used as a standard unit of measurement in trade goods certainly suggests that slaves were an oft-traded commodity among the Celts. Of particular note to language historians is the fact that the Old Irish and Welsh words for 'slave,' cacht and caeth, bear many linguistic similarities with the Latin word for 'slave' or 'captive': captus. This could be taken as a strong suggestion that one of the earliest products traded between the Celtic and Latin cultures was, in fact, slaves.

Thanks to their long running, and well-documented trade partnerships with the Greeks, as well as a preponderance of archaeological evidence, we know that pre-Roman Celtic territories all over Eurasia were crisscrossed with a well-used network of trade routes. Large prehistoric trackways have even been discovered in Ireland and Germany, crossing bogs and spanning substantial distances. Due to their extensive length and width, it has been suggested that these roadways were created for wheeled transport, further enforcing the belief that Celtic traders did a brisk business using carts and wagons, or perhaps other forms of wheeled transport, and may have traveled in caravans for efficiency and protection. We know that the territory controlled and occupied by the Celts contained a wealth of iron, tin, lead, silver and gold. These precious mineral resources were mined and crafted by Celtic smiths and metalworkers into weapons and beautiful pieces of jewelry for trade with their international neighbors; the Romans were frequent buyers of Celtic luxuries and ornamentations.

At some juncture in modern scholarship concerning the Gauls, it was believed that the Celtic monetary system was comprised solely of a barter system that lacked a distinct coinage currency and relied solely on an exchange of goods. This belief has now been proven at least partly false. One reason behind this is that the barter system practiced by the Celts, much like the coinage system developed during the late Roman Empire, was so complex that it is still not fully understood by modern historians. Because the Celts lacked the resources and technology to mass produce a uniform form of currency, it is assumed that they traded with various forms of "proto money." Proto money could have included bronze items in the shape of axe heads, or trinkets like rings and bells. Many of these items have been found in the burial sites of wealthy individuals, suggesting that they were held in high value and frequently used in "day to day" purchases. Celtic metalwork, in particular, was greatly prized for its beauty and intricate detail, and hoarded by those who could afford it.

In addition to these barter items, the Celts did, in fact, employ several forms of currency: low value coinages formed out of potin, a bronze alloy with a high concentration of tin, and higher value coinages minted in gold, silver, or high quality bronze. The Celtic regions of France were so rich in gold that the Celts were able, in fact, to produce an abundance of gold coins and goods to meet the demand for the precious metal in Rome. Unfortunately, this gold fever is thought to be a major reason for why Caesar eventually invaded the French territories of the Celts.

During the reign of Caesar Augustus (reigning from 31 BCE to 14 CE), the Roman Empire had expanded immensely and there was a peaceful trading relationship with the northern Celtic tribes, although there were outbreaks of conflicts. In northern Europe, this period is known as the Roman Iron Age, or the Late Iron age. However, when Augustus had his army try to push the borders of the Roman Empire further towards the River Elbe, his army was completely destroyed by the Celtic tribes, led by the Cherusci chief, Arminius.

This particular defeat of Rome at the hands of the Celtic people is of particular significance. The Romans at this point wielded a much more advanced and disciplined army than what we know about the Celts, and, militarily speaking, the Atlantic Celts have always been regarded as more conservative than the Romans. For example, the Celts were still employing chariots to support infantry surges during wartime engagements; this was at a time when the Greeks and Romans had long confined chariots to exclusive use in entertainment and ceremonial roles. In spite of using this antiquated war machine, the Celts were able to repel even the much more advanced armies of Julius Caesar in later years of conflict.

Although the trading relationship with the south during the Early Iron Age was connected with the trade routes that transported bronze to Scandinavia from central Europe, these stopped during the early pre-Roman Iron Age.

However, when the exchange structure began to start up again, they were used to forge relationships with other Celtic tribes and, as a guarantee of loyalty, connected with the political status, instead of sacrificial or luxury goods.

During the second century CE, the Roman Empire had reached its heights, but the central Germanic Celtic tribes had begun to merge together, creating a strength the Roman Empire couldn't ignore. A number of wars and battles broke out, leading to a mass of Germanic migrations.

In the fourth century CE there was an onslaught of migratory people pushing into Gaul that would lead to the Celtic groups moving westwards and north. In 410 CE, the Goths sacked the city of Rome under the command of Alarik. At the same time, the Romans abandoned Britain and left it open to the Angles and Saxons from northwest Germany and southern Jutland.

It was the last battle Attila the Hun faced in 446 that sealed the Celtic future. He faced an army made up of Visigoths, Franks, Saxons, and Burgundians, and met them on the Catalaunian Plains. However, Attila's forces were destroyed and the Huns disappear from Europe. The Germanic Celtic tribes were now masters of Western Europe and, in 500 CE, King Clovis established the Frankish kingdom.

We have a good amount of knowledge on the various Celtic tribes that lived in Scandinavia circa 500 CE, especially through the historians Jordanes and Procopius. The Screrefennae, also known as Skrithifinoi, were hunter-gatherers, whilst the Swedes, known as the Suehans or Suetidi, were a sedentary society. Other people included the Rygi, who might have lived in present day Norway; the Dani in Denmark and the Finni in Finland.

Certain areas in Celtic Scandinavia became important cultural centers, especially the islands of Oland and Gotland in Norway.

One interesting, and certainly unusual aspect about Ancient Celtic culture concerns the roles of gender and sexual norms within their society. It was the famous philosopher Aristotle who wrote that the "most belligerent nations" were strongly influenced not by their kings, but by the women who had the ear of the king. While that may have been true of many civilizations during Aristotle's time, the Celts were markedly unique in their regard of women and sexual traditions. According to historian H.D. Rankin in his book Celts and the Classical World, many scholars of antiquity seem to foster the general opinion that, while Celtic men did take wives, they openly preferred male lovers. This is supported by the Roman Greek rhetorician Athenaeus, who wrote that "while Celtic women were beautiful, the men preferred to sleep together." Writing in the 1st century BC, another scholarly observer Diodorus Siculus stated that during feasts and gatherings, it was a common sight for young Celtic men to "offer themselves to strangers, and [the young men] are insulted if the offer is refused."

Celtic women themselves enjoyed a great deal of sexual freedom in terms of promiscuity, a fact which was often highlighted by scholars in Rome, a society that at least outwardly fostered monogamous unions and marriages. In a famous conversational exchange noted by Cassius Dio, the wife of a visiting Caledonian leader had met with Julia Augusta, the wife of Augustus Caesar and the Empress of Rome. While their husbands attended to matters of a treaty between their peoples, the Empress made a jest to the Celtic woman in reference to the fact that she was at liberty to engage in sexual intercourse with any man in Britain, even if he was not her husband. The Celtic woman replied, "We fulfill the demands of nature in a much better way than do you Roman women for we consort openly with the best men, whereas you let yourselves be debauched in secret by the vilest."

And the women of the Celtic people were thusly bold not just in boast and conversation, but in battle as well. Very few sources exist that explicitly detail the Celtic view on gender roles and the status of women in society. However, there is a substantial amount of archeological evidence to suggest that Celtic women may have had roles in combat and enjoyed a significantly more egalitarian position in society than women in Rome.

One such piece of evidence, and quite possibly the most famous, has been dubbed the Grave of the Lady of Vix. Located just outside the idyllic village of Vix in northern eastern Burgundy in modern day France, the grave is part of a sprawling 42 hectare necropolis built near what is believed to be the site of a fortified Celtic stronghold, or oppidum. The graves here have interred the dead from the Hallstatt culture from the Late Bronze Age to the Late La Tene, and may have seen burial activity up until the

Late Antiquity period. The area around Vix is the center of a flat plain with highly fertile soil; agriculturally rich, the location was likely the site of an important settlement and trade route destination. This would suggest those who were buried here must have occupied positions of high societal standing.

It was here, in one of several burial mounds, that the Grave of the Lady of Vix was discovered. The grave dates back to circa 500 BC, and what is remarkable about it is that the grave had never been looted, even though it was filled with astoundingly lavish grave offerings. Sometimes collectively termed the Trésor de Vix, the Treasure of the Lady of Vix consistsedof a great amount of fine, masterfully crafted jewelry. The centerpiece of the collection was the Vix krater, a 5'4" (1.63 m) tall vessel used in wine-making. The Vix krater is the largest known metal vessel ever to have been discovered dating back to Western classical antiquity. Most relevant to our current discussion is that, in addition to her lavish jewelry, urns, wine jugs, torcs, friezes, and other ornamental burial goods, the Lady of Vix was also buried with a great quantity of weapons. As well, many of her other grave goods bear engravings ascribing to a military motif: armored hoplites marching to war, chariots, spear-wielders, and a lioness motif features prominently throughout. The presence of these warlike items and symbols, combined with the fact that the Lady of Vix was buried alone, and not alongside a male counterpart, suggests that the ancient Celtic woman must have occupied a prominent and independently wealthy position in society. Some historians have even gone so far as to suggest that the Lady of Vix could have been the celebrated leader of an army in wartime.

Though no written account remains to tell of the life of the Lady of Vix, we do have a great deal of literature written about another famous Celtic woman warrior, Boudica. Commentary by the Roman historian Tacitus describes Boudica as the queen of a Celtic tribe, the Iceni. Upon the death of her husband, Boudica was to have inherited the kingdom, but instead, she found her people annexed by the Romans. After she and her daughters had endured a brutal rape and public flogging, Boudica rallied the Iceni people in a bloody rebellion against their Roman oppressors. The rebels destroyed several Roman outposts and towns. Most noteworthy of all was the 20-year-old colonial Roman settlement of Londinium (modern day London).

Historical accounts report that Boudica led a force of 100,000 Iceni, Trinovantes mercenaries, and others, against a famous Roman Legion, the Legio IX Hispana. Although the Legion was significantly more experienced in combat, having cut their teeth during a long, grueling overland campaign in the Spanish peninsula, it knew it was outmatched. Lacking enough soldiers to defend the settlement, the Romans evacuated as many settlers as they could. Boudica's forces poured into Londinium, destroying the city and slaughtering anyone who failed to heed the evacuation order. The rebels' destruction was so brutal that modern day archeological excavations of the site reveal a thick red layer of dust covering coins, shattered pottery, and disembodied skulls within the bounds of the city. The rebel crisis led by Queen Boudica was so great that it nearly led Emperor Nero to the decision to withdraw all Roman forces and abandon Britain to the Celts. However, the unrelenting Roman onslaught eventually whittled down the rebellion, leading Boudica to commit suicide in order to avoid capture. Today, there are numerous statues of Boudica popularly depicting her riding a horse driven chariot into battle, and the warrior queen is celebrated as a lasting icon representing the strength and courage of Celtic women.

While the Celts received a lot of attention from Greek and later Roman onlookers for allowing women on the battlefield, the actual number of female fighters among the Celts was probably quite low, making the appearance of Celtic warrior women more of an exception rather than a rule. There may have been practical reasons behind fostering a warrior culture among both genders, however, as tribal warfare appears to have been a common enough occurrence among all Celtic societies. Although epic literature often romanticizes brutal tribal conflicts as almost sporting endeavors focused on raids and hunting, rather than abject slaughter, the reality was most likely far bloodier. A number of historical records describe Celtic tribes warring among each other to exert political dominance, to disrupt neighboring or rival clans, and to secure important trade routes or access to resources. In some instances, Celtic tribes warred among each other with the intent to conquer territory.

Irish heroic tales, epics, and songs from the medieval period and during the pre-Christian era depict legendary Celtic warriors, such as the mythical Cú Chulainn, engaging in single combat armed with a spear and javelin. Celtic warrior heroes are never described wearing helmets or metal armor, and chariots are often described as important vehicles of transport and warfare. This is in keeping with archeological findings, so historians have traditionally been inclined to paint a picture of the typical Celtic warrior as light infantry fighting in irregular formations, wearing little armor. Or sometimes, no armor at all.

Indeed, there has been some mention by Roman scholar Polybius that certain Celts fought naked. This claim has been corroborated by a number of archeological findings, such as statuettes and figurines that depict naked Gallic warriors bearing arms into battle. According to Polybius, this spectacle was particularly terrifying to their adversaries, as these Celtic warriors "were all men of splendid physique and in the prime of life." As for weapons, the Celts are described as fighting with both spears and a kind of long-bladed sword used for hacking edgewise, rather than stabbing. Many Celtic swords were made from Noric steel, produced in Celtic Noricum, and the quality and deadliness of this steel became so famous that the Roman Empire later used it to forge the weapons that equipped their

Legions.

In terms of military tactics, we have only the imperfect accounts of their frequent enemies, the Romans, to go on, and so their reliability might have to be questioned. But according to the classical Roman writers such as Strabo, Livy, Pausanias, and Florus, the Celts fought like "wild beasts," in disorganized hordes that adopted "frenzied and erratic postures, quite lacking in military science." Celtic hordes would throw the whole weight of their bodies into a frontal assault, "like hewers of wood or men digging with mattocks," and relied on the strength of their blows and the weight of their numbers to overwhelm their enemies. These descriptions have been challenged by modern day historians. Alas, because the Celts kept few preserved records of their customs and war tactics, we have scarce evidence with which to construct a clearer picture of Celtic military strategy.

Another interesting aspect of Celtic warfare was their reputation among their enemies as head hunters. According to modern historian Paul Jacobsthal, "Amongst the Celts, the human head was venerated above all else, since the head was to the Celt the soul, centre of the emotions as well as of life itself, a symbol of divinity and of the powers of the other world." Several carved illustrations dating back to the La Tene period seem to support this argument, as they depict severed heads. The scarce collection of surviving Celtic mythology spread throughout the centuries contain numerous tales that reference the severed heads of heroes and saints. In fact, it seems to be a common enough motif for particularly virtuous or legendary figures to carry their own severed heads. Take, for example, the famous Arthurian tale Sir Gawain and the Green Knight. Here, the Green Knight, a mysterious and unearthly warrior in green armor, is beheaded by a sword blow from Sir Gawain. The Green Knight later appears in King Arthur's court seated on a horse. He holds aloft his own severed head, which pronounces his intention to test the will and virtue of the Knights of the Round Table.

Similarly, the mythological Irish fairy known as the Dullahan often appears as a headless rider atop a jet black horse. The Dullahan carries his own severed head under one arm, and in his other he wields the spine of a human corpse like a whip. Then there is St. Denis of Paris, who was martyred by being beheaded by a sword. Upon his decapitation, however, St. Denis did not die, but instead knelt down, picked up his head, and walked six miles (10 km) to the top of Montmartre. All the while, his severed head continued to preach a sermon of repentance.

Diodorus Siculus, writing in the 1st Century, describes the Celts as having a peculiar fixation with retrieving the heads of enemy's slain battle. Diodorus purports that these heads were dipped in cedar oil for embalming and then nailed upon the walls of their homes, proudly displayed like animal trophies.

The heads of particularly distinguished enemies were kept in chests and exhibited proudly to visitors. During these displays, the triumphant warrior could be found boasting that he had refused a large sum of money, or the weight of the head in gold, for the purchase or return of this head. Not surprisingly, Diodorus' account has generated controversy in recent years, as has the traditional assumption that the Celts were head hunters. Recent findings in France has suggested that, while the Celts did place a great degree of spiritual significance in the human head, it was the heads of slain allies that were collected for display in porticos; the remains of slain enemies were dumped in mass graves, their weapons broken in a ritual to prevent them from being used again.

But the Celts were not solely savage warrior's intent on perpetuating warfare. Their production of art and masterfully crafted luxury goods was widely celebrated by their neighboring cultures. In academic circles, the term "Celtic art" refers to the art of the La Tene period that flourished across Europe. But popularly, the "Celtic art" known too much of the general public is known as Insular art in art history. Both styles are Celtic, by definition, although they contain considerable influences from sources that are decidedly not Celtic. Nonetheless, the two major Celtic art styles share a preference for symmetrical, geometric ornamentation over figurative or symbolic subjects. Traditional Celtic art also greatly differs from Roman, and later Christian, art, as narrative scenes only appear under outside influence, and even then, are often rendered in extremely stylized manners.

Celtic patterns and artistic forms are often described as energetic, their elegant circular forms creating triskeles and spirals. Celtic artists used a variety of materials to render their art, such as stone, wood, and precious metals. The Celts also developed advanced musical instruments such as the carnyce, a war trumpet believed to have been used before battle to bolster morale and frighten the enemy. Perhaps the most distinguishable style of Celtic art follows the 'interlace' patterns, and formed a characteristic of the whole of the British Isles. These patterns are properly referred to as Insular art, or Hiberno-Saxon art. Celtic artists in metalwork used this style extensively in their creations, and monks used it to illuminate their manuscripts such as the famous Book of Lindisfarne and the Book of Kells.

When the Continental Celts were eventually conquered and subsumed by the Romans, Celtic art adopted many elements of Roman, Greek, and other art styles normally "foreign" to their culture, but some Celtic elements remained popular well into the later medieval period. Indeed, throughout Europe, the Celtic influence in art can be seen in many avenues.

Luxury goods continued to be transported into Celtic Scandinavia, but instead of the Romans, it was the Frankish who Celtic people they were dealing with. Glass and bronze items produced in Belgium and France were particularly favored by the Scandinavian Celts... Gold was highly sought after and was typically melted down and reworked by local craftsmen. Massive gold hoards have been uncovered, particularly in Storegarden and Mone in Sweden and at Farjestaden on Oland.

In the seventh century, there was the establishment of a new practice—boat graves. It has been suggested that these boat graves were to honor the king's close warriors. Those who belonged to this warrior aristocracy typically owned farms and land and would have had great impact in how the establishment of the Swedish state. Iron also played a vital role in the development of the Swedish state, and also highlights the strong trading relationship with the rest of the Celtic world in Britain and Europe.

The Viking Age, between 800 and 1050 CE, was an era of great expansion. There were many reasons why the Vikings from Scandinavia migrated from their homelands. Those in the west went with the traditional view of plunder or colonization, although those in the east established strong trade links with Asia Minor, supplying the market with Baltic goods such as furs, amber, and slaves. In Denmark and Norway, space was becoming a great issue and so they looked to the north British islands, such as Orkney, Shetland, and the Hebrides.

The Vikings had their own pantheon of gods, which had an impact on the religious beliefs of the other Celtic groups they came into contact with, but by 1050 they had finally converted to Christianity.

Chapter 7
Celtic Religion

The ancient Celts as a civilization reached their heights in the fourth century BCE, their territory stretching from Britain all the way to Asia Minor. It was after the third century BCE that their culture started to experience a sharp decline and disintegration, especially in mainland Europe. The decline was much slower in Britain and Ireland, but through political pressures and dominance, the Celtic culture was continually eroded until it faded away. The Celtic languages, belonging to the Indo-European language family, are used in western European fringes today and in limited areas of the British Isles and Brittany in modern day France (the latter is due to a mass migration from Britain between the fourth and seventh centuries CE). As such, it is little wonder then that the chaotic and irregular history of the Celtic culture has influenced the Celtic cultural and religious records.

Sources
Because of the fragmentary and disjointed nature of existing evidence, modern day historians know little for certain about Celtic polytheism. This difficulty is further compounded by the

fact that the Celts who practiced this religion wrote absolutely nothing down about their spiritual beliefs and ritual customs. There are, however, two key sources that give us our knowledge on Celtic religion—the first are the sculptural monuments that were created by the Celts living in Britain and continental Europe, and secondly, the limited amount of Celtic literature which was penned during the medieval period and has survived from this era. However, despite these two key resources, interpreting them can be challenging. The majority of the monuments and their inscriptions date back to the Roman period and mirror a significant degree of syncretism between the Roman pantheon and the Celtic one.

In addition, even when the gods or motifs do look as though they predate the Roman occupation, it can be a challenge to interpret them when there is a lack of surviving writings on Celtic religion. This fact has made it particularly challenging to interpret these monuments and inscriptions; no matter how elaborate or beautiful the motifs, we are essentially still lacking the tabula rasa, the cipher needed to decode them. Where the Celtic figures and motifs appear to have a point of origin that predates the Roman tradition, they have proven extremely difficult to interpret without any sort of foreknowledge or preserved literature on mythology. One example that has proven particularly vexing to modern day scholars is the presence of a horned deity called Cernunnos. Cernunnos is attested to by name only once, but his likeness appears all over Gaul and even as far away among the artwork of Celtiberians—the Celtic speaking peoples of the Iberian Peninsula. Cernunnos is depicted as a human with the antlers of a stag, sometimes a purse filled with coins, and is often seated cross legged and holding or wearing a torc. Beyond his familiar appearance and apparent popularity among the Celts, historians know nothing about Cernunnos. Specific and accurate details about his name, his followers, the legends and myths attributed to him, and his significance to the Celtic pantheon are, at least for the moment, utterly lost to time.

It was only after a considerable amount of time that had passed, starting in the 7th century CE in Ireland and much later in Wales, that the myths and legends of the Celts were written down. At this point in time, the people of Ireland and Wales had been converted to Christianity and the ones who were writing the legends down were monks. As such, the literature that has survived from this time is diverse and plentiful, but is quite displaced in period and in setting from its epigraphic and illustrative counterparts from mainland Europe and mirrors the audience's discrimination and much of its Christian education. Taking these points into consideration, it is still somewhat amazing that there are numerous agreements between the limited writings and the inscriptions found in continental Europe. We see this particularly in the writings of Classical authors such as Poseidonius who penned both theirs and other people's views on the Celts.

Various other archaeological discoveries have helped advance our understanding of the religion practiced by the Celts.

From these sources, we know that the Celts, like other European tribal societies during the Iron Age, practiced a form of religion that was polytheistic, meaning that they believed in a pantheon of gods instead of one all-powerful being. The Celts were also animists, believing that all natural things—even animals and inanimate objects, such as rocks, trees, and mountains—were either possessed of a soul or were capable of housing a spirit, and thus, were deserving of veneration and respect.

One thing that distinguished the Celts from the religions of similar polytheistic cultures was that where, say, the Romans worshiped a pantheon of a dozen or so gods and goddesses, the Celts venerated hundreds of deities. Most of these deities were deeply personal to a single family or tribe, and virtually unknown outside the household, family, or extended tribal lineage. Other gods were more popular and commanded followers that crossed the barriers of both language and culture.

Like the gods and goddesses themselves, Celtic religious patterns, practices, and customs varied from region to region. Some similarities, however, can be seen. For instance, all branches of the Celtic culture worshipped both male and female deities. Male Celtic deities were representative of a particular skill or set of skills. Goddesses, on the other hand, were associated with natural features, and many natural landmarks, particularly rivers, were believed to be inhabited or represented by a particular goddesses, such as how the goddess Boann represented the River Boyne. However, there were exceptions. Some goddesses, such as Brighid and The Morrigan, were associated with both natural features such as holy wells and the River Unius, and manual skills such as blacksmithing and healing.

Another similarity seen among the religious beliefs of the Celtic people is the theme of triplicity: A number of important deities appeared in sets of three, or were otherwise depicted as threefold. One well-known example is the Three Mothers, a group of goddesses worshiped by several prominent Celtic tribes. Though each tribe had its own regional variation on the appearance, nature, and symbolism associated with these spiritual figures, they are always represented as the *Three* Mothers, always appearing as a trio.

According to Roman reports, the druids were the principal priests, figures of religious authority in the Celtic tradition. In their society, druids filled a variety of religious roles, serving as priests and religious officials, and, in some accounts, druids were also called to be judges. They were teachers, keepers of lore, and the conductors of sacrifices. Naturally, it fell upon the druids to organize and host religious ceremonies, and they were relied upon for their memorization of the calendar. Druids themselves had their own internal class system, and certain classes of druids were tasked with carrying out ceremonial sacrifices of crops or livestock in order to appease unruly gods, or to otherwise better their communities. Druids were purportedly observed congregating in sacred groves, where they held their ceremonies. From archeological findings, we know that the druids in service of the La Tene Celts constructed temples of different sizes and shapes, and that they also kept shrines at the sites of what were believed to be sacred trees and votive pools.

The Celts and Animism

It is thought that the pagan Celts perceived that the supernatural was all around them, and that spirits and divine beings inhabited all aspects of the natural world. In contrast with the polytheistic cultures of ancient Greece, and later Rome, which focused on urban life and the belief in a pantheon of gods that were intensely socially structured, the landscape of ancient Celtic spirituality was prominently rural. This is evidenced by the fact that Celtic shrines were often built in remote places, far away from the busy sights and bustling noises of civilization. The Celts believed that every mountain, river, spring, rocky outcrop, marsh, and forest was, or could be endowed, with its own unique spiritual being. It is important to note that the ancient Celts drew few distinctions between "spirit" and "deity"; some animistic beings were referred to interchangeably as gods and goddesses themselves, or as spirits, or as messengers and emissaries of the gods.

Water, in particular, held a special place in Celtic animism. According to Anne Ross, the spirits belonging to watery places garnered particular reverence as givers of life. Waters were also seen as the bridges between the physical realm and the Otherworld. Rivers, springs, hot springs, holy wells, and lakes in particular were highly venerated. The goddess Sequana appears to have embodied the spring at the source of the River Seine, and Sulis was often associated with the hot spring at Bath, Somerset. And Brighid, a major goddess among many Celtic tribes, was said to be manifest in a number of holy wells across Gaulish lands. Water was also held in high esteem as a life-giving force, its healing properties celebrated by the association of the goddess Sulis at Aquae Sulis, and the goddess Arnemetia at Aquae Arnemetiae, both settlements located at the site of natural hot springs. Archeological evidence that the pre-Roman Iron Age Celts were particularly worshipful of watery places can be found in the abundance of special offerings at lakes, rivers, springs and bogs. Often, remains of metalwork, wooden objects, and animals are found at this site—and occasionally, the remains of human beings.

Particularly sacred sites included the earth and, naturally, waters where the dead were buried; these places were imbued with particular sanctity and were treated as holy sites often visited by living relatives to pay respects or to leave offerings to the departed. Sanctuaries were other sacred places believed to be separated from the world of the mundane and all its trials and ills, often to be found in natural locations such as mountain springs, sacred groves, and hidden woodland lakes. Finally, particularly impressive topographical features, such as mountain peaks and ridges, were regarded as abodes of powerful spirits and deities. In order to form a desirable link between these places and spirits, Celtic clansmen were encouraged to leave offerings of food, weapons, or even jewelry at these sites.

Like many Iron Age peoples, the Celtic culture was fascinated and inspired by meteorological patterns and weather phenomena. In particular, the yearly cycles of wind, rain, and thunder captured the imaginations of early Celts. From Roman era inscriptions, we know that several noteworthy Celtic spirits were associated with these powerful natural forces. In particular, Taranis the 'Thunderer' was not simply the god of thunder, but he *was* thunder. Both awe inspiring and dreadful to behold, lightning and thunder gave rise to the dual nature of Taranis as both a majestic and savage god who demanded human sacrifice. It is believed that the Romans derived their own thunder god, Jupiter, from a merging of the native Celtic deity Taranis with a physical appearance that resembled a man in Roman garb. Likewise, the Cailleachan were Scottish storm hags, and the Cailleach herself brought the first winter snows to the land when she washed her great plaid garment in a whirlpool. When she had finished, her plaid was the pure white snow that blanketed the land.

Trees were also held in high regard in the pantheon of Celtic animistic spirits. According to Celtic tradition, trees had spirits, and certain trees were inhabited by particularly wise and potent spirits. The most sacred of all trees in Ireland were the ancient bíle trees that often formed the heart of a Celtic village. Many settlements were built around these trees, which served as the social and ceremonial meeting place for the tribe. At one time, there were five sacred bíles of Ireland, corresponding to the five Irish provinces that existed during that time: the Ash of Tortu, the Bole of Ross, the Oak of Mugna, and the Ash of Dathi.

Again sharing similarities with other animistic religions, both the Continental and Insular Celts were greatly interested in the behavior of animals and birds. Migration patterns were intently observed throughout the year for omens and portents of events to come, and spirits were closely attributed to certain animals. In Ireland, the Morrigan, a major goddess queen entrusted with the power of foretelling doom and death in battle, was often associated with a variety of beasts, in particular the crow. In Scotland, the goddess Brighid was said to be able to shift between various animal forms, such as snakes and cattle.

Creatures did not necessarily have to have a spirit attached to them, but could simply be admired for the qualities they represented to the Celts. Beavers were seen to be skillful woodworkers, and thus held in high esteem by woodcarvers. Dogs were regarded as masterful hunters and guardians, and horses and stags were greatly respected for their beauty, speed and virility. Snakes were seen as representations of longevity, due in part to their ability to shed their skin and renew themselves. A similar attribute was given to deer, who in shedding their antlers, go through several cycles of growth and renewal.

The Celtic Gods

The classical source for our understanding on the Celtic gods in mainland Europe comes from Julius Caesar's *The Gallic War*. In his writings he tells of five Celtic deities and what their roles were. Using Roman names for them, Mercury was the most widely worshipped of all the Celtic deities, and there were many images of him. He was believed to be the creator of all the arts, and the protector of travelers and traders, as well as being the most authoritative deity when it came to grain and trade. The next gods to be worshipped were Apollo, Minerva, Mars, and Jupiter; as with the Roman pantheon, these gods held similar functions (i.e. Jupiter ruling the heavens, and Mars as a war god, etc.).

In typical Roman fashion, Caesar didn't use the local names for these Celtic gods. Instead, he used the names of their Roman counterparts. This makes it harder for us to determine the Celtic gods in the limited written sources, rather than that of the Roman deities. In addition to this, Caesar also put forth a well-ordered representation comparison of the deity and their role which was quite strange compared to the vernacular historical evidence. Despite its limitations, the short catalog of deities is quite a valued resource and a precise observation. When we compare his accounts to that of other historical writings or the inscriptions found on monuments throughout Celtic lands, Caesar's accounts and the iconography actually refer to the various points in Celtic history—that the motifs dating to the Roman period belong to a setting where there was great social and governmental upheavals and the religious views it illustrates could have been much more chaotic than that preserved by the priests and druids when Gaul was an independent region.

In comparison, the apparent absence of structure in Celtic religion can be more deceptive than real. From the sources that have survived we have the names or identities of more than 700 Celtic gods from Gaul, but the bulk of these names were only mentioned a single time. This has led to the theory that, instead of being a widespread and official pantheon, the Celtic gods were worshipped on a local basis. The scholars who back this theory reference Lucan's reference to a deity named Teutates, which has been suggested to mean 'god of the tribe' (*teuta* is believed to be translates as tribe in the Celtic language). The assortment of names could also be attributed to being epithets or titles used by major deities worshipped throughout the Celtic world. The belief of the Celtic pantheon as simply as an abundance of native deities is challenged by numerous well-demonstrated gods whose venerations were celebrated nearly all over the Celtic world.

From Caesar's accounts on his campaigns in Gaul, the most venerated deity was 'Mercury,' and we can confirm this through inscriptions and other archaeological evidence. Although Caesar didn't mention his Celtic name directly, it is implied through the location name of Lugudunon, which translates as the dwelling of the god Lugus. His major places of worship were centered in present day Laon, Loudun and Lyon in France, and Leiden in the Netherlands. His counterpart in Ireland was Lugh, Lleu in Wales, and all had similar customs to the worship of Lugus in continental Europe. Lugus' man epithet was 'possessed of many talents', which could explain why Caesar referred to him as the creator of all the arts. When we look at the Battle of Magh Tuiredh, an ancient Irish myth, Lugh tells of how he is the chief of all the arts. Indeed, even in ancient inscriptions found in modern day Spain and Switzerland honor the god in both singular and triple aspect.

When we look at a collection of stories known as the Mabinogion, we can clearly see a relationship with making shoes, showing Lleu (the Welsh version of Lugus) as a highly skilled shoemaker. Back in Ireland, Lugh was able to overcome the evil Balar, the heavenly archetype of sacred kingship, and his other most widely used title was 'of the long arm' which highlights an ancient Indo-European reference for a king spreading his dominance and authority over wide regions. His main celebration was known as the Festival of Lugh and was held during the month of August (and is still held even today); the archaeological record shows that two of the earliest locations for these celebrations were said to be the eternal resting places for goddesses connected with the fertility of the earth.

"Mars," another highly venerated Celtic deity, shows us just how challenging it is to link the Roman and Celtic gods with each other. There is a well-known section in the *Bellum Civile*, written by Lucan, which tells how the Celts would offer gory sacrifices in honor of three deities—Teutates, Taranis, and Esus. One later writer associates Teutates with the Roman god Mercury, whereas another links him with Mars. One reason behind this clear confusion—highlighted in other areas as well—is that the deities belonging to the Celtic cultures were not tightly catalogued or classified in their roles and identities. As such, 'Mercury' could well be known as king of the gods, but might also be classed as a warrior; whereas 'Mars' could be a defender of the community and, because of this, could be identified with Teutates.

The challenge of identifying these characters, associations, and roles is emphasized in the example of the Celtic version of Apollo--he had more than 15 titles, but they could have been the names of different gods from various locations. Belenus' connection with the sun (the Celtic translation for 'shining') would have reinforced the association with the Classical god Apollo. Other titles such as Grannus (meaning boiling) would link him with the art of healing, particularly when it came to the healing properties of thermal springs—a location that was thought to have great spiritual belief in the ancient world, a belief that some still retain today. Maponos (the Divine Son) is demonstrated in continental Europe but is widely seen in the north of Britain. In Medieval Wales, he was known as Mabon—his most popular legend tells of how the baby deity was stolen from his mother when he was just three days old. Later on, he was known as Mabuz and Mabonagrain in the Arthur legends. In Ireland, his counterpart was Mac ind Og (Young Son), also called Oenghus. He was said to have lived in Bruigh na Boinne, the passage grave known as Newgrange which pre-dates the Celtic culture. His father was the king god of the Irish people, Dagda, and Boann, the embodiment of the holy river. In ancient writings, he was considered to be a crafty character and enjoyed a reputation as a great lover.

The Celtic equivalent to 'Minerva' (or Athena in the Greek pantheon) was widely worshipped, with inscriptions and dedications found to her throughout the Celtic world. In Britain, the most famous site of her worship was at the town of Bath, where she was merged with the local goddess Sulis, whose veneration was celebrated at the thermal springs. She was considered to be one of the most important mother goddesses and her plural name of Suleviae illustrates this role, as many mother goddesses were depicted in triple form. In Ireland, her counterpart was Brighid, who was the child of Dagda. Just as with Minerva, Brighid was believed to be associated with healing and arts, but in addition to this, she was considered the goddess of traditional education. Her name is similar to the guardian goddess of the Brigantes of modern day England, Briganti. There are strong indications that her worship was transferred from Continental Europe when the Brigantes journeyed to Britain and then Ireland.

The Continental European Celtic god Sucellos, whose name might be translated as the Good Striker, materializes on numerous statues and reliefs, typically holding a mallet in his hand. He was identified with the Irish deity Dagda and was also known as Eochaidh Ollathair. In this role, his characteristics include the cauldron of plenty and a club. Ireland also had a sea god known as Manannan mac Lir, as well as a primeval deity named Thethra who we know very little about, but on mainland Europe there has been no proof to suggest that there was a sea god from this region. This could be because, as the primary motherland of the Celtic people was a non-coastal area, there was no need for a sea god.

The limited amount of written accounts we have illustrate how individual gods were connected with certain craftworks. Vulcan, the Roman god of metalwork (Hephaestus in the Greek pantheon) was incredibly well-known; despite Caesar not telling us of one, we known that there was a Celtic version of Vulcan and was extremely popular. In Ireland he was known as Goibhniu; in Wales he was called Gofannon—in both these cases, his name originates for the Celtic word smith. Goibhniu, together with other smith gods, created deadly weapons which had a reputation for always hitting their targets. In addition to this, he was considered a great healing deity and, as Gobban, a common name of his, a magnificent builder.

Goddesses and Divine Consorts

One particular aspect we see quite a lot in Celtic monuments is the unification of male and female (for example, that of 'Mercury' and Rosmerta). Simply speaking, they mirror the togetherness of the guardian god of the community and that of the mother goddess who guaranteed the continuation of the land's fertility. It is not possible to differentiate precisely amongst the individual goddesses and the mother goddesses, who were known as matres. These mother goddesses were typically portrayed in triple form in Celtic depictions. However, both styles of goddesses were connected with fertility and nature's seasons. When we look at the evidence at hand, it is clear that they both originate from the worship of one goddess, the great mother of all.

In the myths and legends from Wales and Irelands we can clearly see the various aspects to the goddesses' personalities. In these stories, the goddesses will typically take on a different personality or character entirely, an opposite role. In one case, the goddess may be portrayed as a lovely and charming woman, the personification of rightful kingship with her monarch, but then she might also be old, ugly, and haggard when she doesn't have a king. Another role may see her as the embodiment of the horrors of war, such as the Morrigan, but then take on the role of the divine journeyman who ventures to the Netherlands with the brave hero. In her role as a life-giver, she was typically associated with rivers and other watery areas.

It is the Celtic reaction of this primeval mother goddess who gives life and fertility to the world through her relationship with a father deity which brings about the character of the goddesses themselves. Celtic legends from Wales and Ireland show a triadic bond between mother, father, and son.

Zoomorphic Deities

Interestingly, the Celtic peoples did not begin attributing human shapes to their deities until the late Iron Age. When they did, they tended to incorporate animal features into their humanized gods. These half-human, half-animal gods were often venerated as deities of the hunt, and symbolized an acknowledgment of the importance of animals to both the survival and economy of the community as a whole. Nature was, to the Celts, a force to be revered and awed, but also to be harvested for the well-being of the tribe. These hunter gods were venerated particularly among the Continental Celts and seemed to occupy a dual role as protectors of both the hunter and the hunted, a tendency that has been likened to the Roman view of Diana and Artemis, both goddesses of the hunt in their own right. Examples of Celtic hunter gods can be found in Gaul, where an armed and antlered hunter god lays his hands on his stag companion. In Le Touget in Gers, a different hunter god tenderly cradles a dying hare in his arms, and in the Ardennes, we see Arduinna, the boar goddess, astride her ferocious wild boar, holding her knife aloft. Naturally, the Celts may have viewed the hunt itself as a symbolic and sacred ritual as much as it was a practical activity for garnering sustenance. The Greek writer Arrian, writing in the 2nd Century CE, stated that the Celts never went hunting without the blessing and permission of the gods. And if they were fortunate enough to garner prey, it was expected that they make a sacrifice of a domestic animal as a form of reparation for removing a wild creature from the natural order.

There is a wonderful array of animals depicted in Celtic monuments, illustrating the gods and goddesses in different combinations of both human and animalistic shapes, and this is found additionally in the limited writings we have. The Horned

One, also known as Cernunnos, is the most common representation of this feature of Celtic religious belief, but there is only one written reference to it. The world-renowned Gundestrup Cauldron, which dates back to the first century BCE, shows Cernunnos in a yoga-type seating position (somewhat similar to that of the Hindu god Siva) with antlers on his head. In both cases, the deity shows his role as a master or lord of the animals.

The bull is widely found in Celtic religion, known as the Brown Bull of Cooley. This heavenly bull is a main character in the Tain Bo Cuailnge, a heroic story from Ireland, and tells of the Bull of the Three Cranes, of which depictions show on the cathedrals of Trier and Notre Dame de Paris. Scholars believe that this legend originates back in Continental Europe but has vanished.

There are a number of various animals which play vital roles in Celtic religion. These include bears, horses, and dogs. The horse was incredibly important and the goddess Epona, whose name originates as Horse Goddess, illustrates the relationship between animal and Celtic people. Her worship originates far in the east and was spread to the west, reaching the shores of Britain. She was worshipped by the Romans and even brought to Rome. In Ireland, she was associated with the goddess Edain Echraidhe and Rhiannon in Wales.

The Celtic Otherworld

In Celtic mythology, the Otherworld is the realm of spirits and, possibly, also the dead. To the Gauls of Britain, the Otherworld was elusive, distinct, and hidden from the mortal plane. It was in itself a supernatural place of everlasting youth, beauty, and abundance. At times, the Otherworld crossed over with the living world; this crossing was signaled by phenomena such as a sudden and abrupt mist, sudden changes in the weather, or the presence of divine beings, spirit messengers, or animals with unusual features. In many legends, a woman of unearthly beauty offered the hero an apple or a silver apple branch, or a ball of thread that unwound. These were often invitations to enter the Otherworld. Often, the hero would accept and sail away with the woman on a boat made of glass, in a war chariot, or on an enchanted horse galloping over the water. Sometimes, neither the hero nor the woman were ever seen again; in others, the hero returned after what he believed to be a short time, only to find that all his companions had died in battle or from old age, because he had been gone for over a hundred years. Other ways of reaching the Otherworld might be found by entering ancient burial mounds, exploring deep caves, or crossing the western sea. The Otherworld could also be reached by diving into the deep waters of pools, lakes, or the sea.

While there are many legends that tell of mortals crossing into the Otherworld, scholars of mythology are unsure if it represents the final destination of the dead. In Irish myth, there is mention of another unearthly realm called Tech Duinn, the "House of the Dark One." It is believed that this was the destination of the dead: their souls would travel to the House of the Dark One, there to remain forever, or perhaps as a kind of purgatory on their way to the Otherworld, or to be reincarnated in a different form. Tech Duinn is most frequently identified with Bull Rock, an islet off the west coast of Ireland that bears a striking, if not haunting, resemblance to a megalithic portal tomb. Other Irish myths claimed that the souls of the dead departed west, across the sea, in pursuit of the setting sun.

According to Roman scholar Lucan, the druids of Gaul believed that the souls of the dead went to an Otherworld, which Lucan calls by the Latin name *Orbis alius*, before eventually being reincarnated.

The Otherworld of the ancient Gauls captured the interest of Byzantine scholars as well. One such scholar, Procopius of Caesarea, described a Gaulish rendition of the Otherworld as being located far to the west of Great Britain. According to his scholarship in the myths of the Continental Celtic cultures, Procopius suggested that, upon death, the souls separated from the body and floated to the northwestern coast of Gaul. There, the ghosts would knock desperately at the doors of fishermen, rousing them from their beds. It was the duty of the fishermen, at that point, to ferry their souls across the Channel in ghostly ships, so that they might continue their long journey to the afterlife.

Conclusion

Hopefully by now you have read through this book and have a better understanding of what runes are, where they came from, and what they hold in terms of meaning. While this is a lot of information for you to absorb, you will want to take this book as a starting point and use it to help expand your knowledge of runes. You will soon discover that, beyond writing, runes have a lot of other useful purposes and can be useful in helping you to get a handle on your life.

The history of runes. As you have been shown, is a vibrant and rich one that has a lot of its roots in Norse gods. While many people have long since stop using the writing style of runes in place of a better system, there are a large number of descendants of the Scandinavian people who still use runes as their way of writing and who are very happy with this system just as their ancestors were all those years ago.

If a person wants to be connected with the power of the runes, they will need to know all of the history and mythology that goes along with each of the runes. This is crucial in order to make sure that you are getting the full, true meaning behind all of these runes.

While the history of these dates back to beginning forms of writing, there is the issue that you need to make sure that you know that there are those that associate these with magic. Many people have the feeling that these offer a wide range of powers in helping to direct a person along the path that they are currently on.

Check Out My Other Books

Below you'll find some of my other popular books that are popular on Amazon and Kindle as well. Simply click on the links below to check them out. Alternatively, you can visit my author page on Amazon to see other work done by me.

- My Other Book 'Tarot: The Ultimate Beginners Guide for Learning the Secrets of Tarot Cards'- This Is My Other Book on Amazon

- 'Tarot: The Advanced Guide for Learning the Secrets of Tarot Cards'

- 'Manifesting: The Complete Guide to the Law of Attraction to 'Manifest' the Life You Want'

- 'Wicca: The Ultimate Beginner's Guide to Learning Spells & Witchcraft'

- 'The Ultimate Guide to Breaking Up: How to Break Up Gracefully and Move On'

If the links do not work for whatever reason, you can simply search for these titles on the Amazon website to find them.

We hope you like it!

We really hope that you enjoyed the quality of this book! Now that you read all the content in this book, is there anything that you'd like to let us know?

It would be very very helpful in case you could leave a review directly at Amazon, that would help us publishers and authors to get our books into the hands of other readers.

Please simply follow the link to leave a review
https://www.amazon.com/review/create-review?asin=B00WRHM9R6#

Thank you

Made in the USA
Lexington, KY
29 September 2017